USDA

Un ted States Department of Agr cu ture

Photographic Guidance for Selecting Flow Resistance Coefficients in High-Gradient Channels

Steven E. Yochum, Francesco Comiti, Ellen Wohl,
Gabrielle C. L. David, Luca Mao

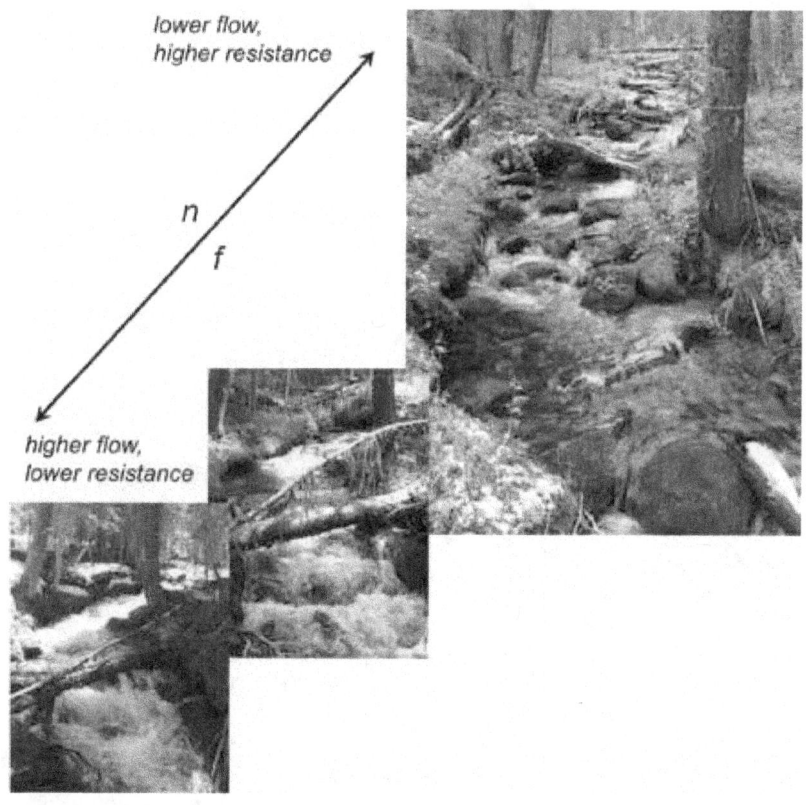

lower flow,
higher resistance

n

f

higher flow,
lower resistance

Forest
Serv ce

Rocky Mounta n
Research Stat on

Genera Techn ca Report
RMRS-GTR-323

Ju y 2014

Yochum, Steven E.; Comiti, Francesco; Wohl, Ellen; David, Gabrielle C. L.; Mao, Luca. 2014. **Photographic Guidance for Selecting Flow Resistance Coefficients in High-Gradient Channels.** Gen. Tech. Rep. RMRS-GTR-323. Fort Collins, CO: U.S. Department of Agriculture, Forest Service, Rocky Mountain Research Station. 91 p.

Abstract

Photographic guidance is presented to assist with the estimation of Manning's n and Darcy-Weisbach f in high-gradient plane-bed, step-pool, and cascade channels. Reaches both with and without instream wood are included. These coefficients are necessary for the estimation of reach-average velocity, energy loss, and discharge. Using data collected in 19 stream channels located in the State of Colorado and the Eastern Italian Alps, on slopes ranging from 2.4 to 21 percent, guidance is provided for low through bankfull flows. Guidance for low flow resistance estimation is additionally provided using data collected in 29 channels in the State of Washington, New Zealand, Chile, and Argentina. Bankfull n values range from 0.048 to 0.30 and low flow n values range from 0.057 to 0.96. Discussions of flow resistance mechanisms and quantitative prediction tools are also presented.

Contents

Nomenclature

A = reach average flow area (m^2)

d = residual

$\overline{d}$ = average residual

D_c = roughness height (m)

d_{84} = bed material size for which 84% of the material is finer (mm)

f = reach average Darcy-Weisbach roughness coefficient (dimensionless)

Fr = Froude number = $V/\sqrt{g\overline{h}}$ (dimensionless)

g = acceleration due to gravity = 9.81 m/s^2

$\overline{h}$ = reach average, average flow depth (m)

h_m = median flow depth, computed from thalweg longitudinal profile (m)

h_L = head loss from flow resistance (m) = $S_f{*}L$

L = thalweg reach length (m)

n = reach average Manning's roughness coefficient (s/m$^{1/3}$)

n = number of measurements

P = system pressure (N/m^2)

P_w = reach average wetted perimeter (m)

Q = flow discharge (m^3/s)

R = reach average hydraulic radius = A/P_w (m)

S = reach slope, typically assumed to be equivalent to the water surface slope (m/m)

S_f= friction slope (m/m)

V = reach average velocity (m/s), measured via tracer travel time and flow path length

v = average section velocity (m/s)

W = reach average flow width (m)

z = elevation (m)

α = velocity head correction factor (dimensionless)

γ = specific weight of the fluid (N/m^3)

σ_z = standard deviation of the residuals of a bed profile regression (m)

Introduction

Practitioners are oftentimes required to predict flow resistance coefficients, such as Manning's n, in high-gradient channels (slopes > ~2 %). Measurements of actual velocity and flow resistance indicate that reach-average resistance coefficients are substantially higher than commonly encountered in low-gradient channels, with Manning's n typically falling between 0.1 to 0.3 for bankfull flows in step-pool and cascade channels (Yochum and others 2012) and flow resistance increasing with decreasing discharge (Lee and Ferguson 2002, Comiti and others 2007, Reid and Hickin 2008, David and others 2010, Yochum and others 2012). Photographic guides for visual comparison with actual channels (Barnes 1967, Aldridge and Garrett 1973, Arcement and Schneider 1989, Hicks and Mason 1998, Coon 1998, Phillips and Ingersoll 1998) provide assistance for estimating these values in lower-gradient channels, but little assistance has been available for high-gradient streams. The selection of appropriate resistance coefficients is essential for improved confidence in hydraulic modeling, stream assessments, stream restoration design, geomorphic analysis, and ecological studies.

Cascade and step-pool channels are relatively stable channel forms with high ratios of sediment transport capacity to sediment supply (Montgomery and Buffington 1997). Cascade channels are characterized by flow that is continuously tumbling, with jets and wakes over and around large clasts and wood features, whereas step-pool channels are characterized by a regular series of channel-spanning steps formed from clasts alone or in combination with in-channel wood. Plane-bed reaches have minimal bedforms, although small-scale bed variability can still be evident. Transitional reaches reflect the wide range in transitional forms between plane-bed, step-pool, and cascade morphologies. Instream wood is often a substantial contributor to flow resistance in these stream types. Step-forming wood contributes substantially to both form and spill resistance, due to wood increasing step heights (David and others 2011).

The Manning equation (Manning 1891) is the most common approach used by practitioners for estimating velocity and energy loss in streams. However, it is considered by some workers to be a poor method for velocity prediction (Ferguson 2010), due to variability by stage and non-dimensionless form. However, Manning's n is the preferred method for prediction by many practitioners and is the method most typically coded into computational models. The Darcy-Weisbach equation (Darcy 1854, Weisbach 1865) is a dimensionless alternative argued to be more appropriate, though it is less commonly used in application and also varies by discharge (Comiti and others 2007, Reid and Hickin 2008, David and others 2010, Yochum and others 2012). The Manning and Darcy-Weisbach equations are:

$$V = \frac{R^{2/3} S_f^{1/2}}{n} = \sqrt{\frac{8gRS_f}{f}} \tag{1}$$

where V is the reach-average velocity (m/s); n is the Manning's roughness coefficient; f is the Darcy-Weisbach friction factor; S_f is the friction slope (m/m); g is the acceleration due to gravity; R, the hydraulic radius, is computed as A/P_w; A is the cross-sectional area (m^2); and P_w is the wetted perimeter (m). In practice, R is often assumed to be the mean depth, though this assumption is only valid for wide channels (width/depth ratio > ~20). In this report, the flow resistance coefficients n and f represent reach-average conditions, with all the terms being reach-averaged values; as such, these coefficients are composite values that include all resistance components within the reach.

The appropriate selection of Manning's n and Darcy-Weisbach f typically depends upon a sufficient level of user experience with the stream type in question. Using guides intended for lower gradient channels, practitioners commonly underpredict flow resistance when estimating resistance coefficients for high-gradient channels. Resistance coefficient underestimation can lead to substantially overestimated flow velocities, underestimated travel times, the miscategorization of reach-average flow regime (subcritical versus supercritical flow), and instability in computational models. Steps and cascades in high-gradient channels, as well as instream wood, all contribute to increased flow resistance. Submergence of these resistance elements causes enhanced variability by stage, further complicating estimation procedures. Hence, there is a need for guidance tools for selecting resistance coefficients in high-gradient channels, and to provide examples for streams with steps, cascades, instream wood, and discharge variability.

"The principal objective of this report is to provide a photographic guide to assist users in the selection of reach-average values of the flow resistance coefficients n and f in high-gradient plane-bed, transitional, step-pool and cascade channels, both with and without instream wood. Values are provided for multiple discharges to illustrate the variation in flow resistance by stage, with additional guidance given for resistance measured during only one discharge. Initially, the methodologies used in the data collection are presented, followed by a section discussing flow resistance mechanisms and quantitative prediction methods in steep streams. These are followed by separate sections presenting photographs and coefficient estimates derived for multiple and single flow levels."

Overview of Field Sites

Photographic guidance is provided based on data collected in North and South America as well as Europe and New Zealand. These channels are relatively small headwater streams; channel characteristics are provided (Tables 1 and 2). Cascade and step-pool streams are the primary channel types, although plane-bed and transitional reaches are also illustrated. The streams included in this report are A, B, C, and F type channels in the Rosgen classification system (Rosgen 1996), with beds dominated by gravel, cobbles, or boulders. Data included in this photographic guide include the results of fieldwork performed in the Southern Rocky Mountains of Colorado, USA (David and others 2010, Yochum and others 2012), the Cascade Mountains of Washington State, USA

Table 1: Range of average channel characteristics, multiple discharge reaches.

	Flow Magnitude	Slope (m/m)	Width (m)	Velocity (m/s)	*n*	*f*
Fraser Experimental Forest	low	0.019 - 0.17	0.67 - 3.3	0.12 - 0.40	0.10 - 0.52	1.4 - 47
	moderate	0.015 - 0.18	0.92 - 4.0	0.18 - 0.61	0.078 - 0.40	0.76 - 26
	~bankfull	0.024 - 0.20	1.1 - 4.0	0.51 - 1.3	0.048 - 0.30	0.28 - 11
Rio Cordon	low	0.079 - 0.21	1.9 - 4.1	0.25 - 0.39	0.18 - 0.41	5.0 - 28
	moderate	0.079 - 0.18	3.5 - 4.2	0.48 - 0.64	0.16 - 0.25	3.9 - 8.3
	high	0.079 - 0.21	3.8 - 5.8	0.5 - 1.6	0.12 - 0.35	0.50 - 1.6

Table 2: Range of average channel characteristics, single discharge reaches.

	Slope (m/m)	Width (m)	Velocity (m/s)	*n*	*f*
Cascades	0.051 - 0.18	0.94 - 3.2	0.079 - 0.25	0.25 - 0.96	11 - 152
Chili and Argentina	0.022 - 0.15	2.8 - 5.3	0.12 - 0.77	0.059 - 0.87	0.50 - 118
New Zealand	0.003 - 0.19	1.6 - 29	0.25 - 0.81	0.021 - 0.36	0.049 - 23

(MacFarlane and Wohl 2003, Curran and Wohl 2003), the Eastern Italian Alps (Comiti and others 2007), the Chilean Araucania (Comiti and others 2008), the Argentine Tierra del Fuego (Comiti and others 2008), and New Zealand's Southern Alps (Wohl and Wilcox 2005). This aggregated dataset includes alluvial channels without instream wood (MacFarlane and Wohl 2003, Comiti and others 2007, Wohl and Wilcox 2005), alluvial channels with instream wood (Curran and Wohl 2003, Comiti and others 2008, David and others 2010, Yochum and others 2011), mixed alluvial and bedrock channels (MacFarlane and Wohl 2003, Curran and Wohl 2003, David and others 2010, Yochum and others 2012), and bedrock channels (MacFarlane and Wohl 2003). Hence, these data were collected in channels with alluvial, mixed alluvial and bedrock, and bedrock beds, both with and without instream wood present and enhancing step heights.

Methodology

Measured values of both Manning's *n* and the Darcy-Weisbach *f* are presented (in the **Photographic Guidance – Multiple Discharges** section and in Appendices A & B), as well as the reach-average slope (S), width (W), length (L), reach-average velocity (V), and hydraulic radius (R). Where available, the discharge (Q) and reach-average Froude number (Fr) are also quantified. These values were computed using flow travel time measurements, longitudinal profiles, and cross-section data. The presented *n* and *f* coefficients were computed from these reach-average values. In channels where resistance at multiple flows was measured, photographs of the low-, medium-, and ~bankfull-flow conditions are provided. In channels where resistance was measured at only one flow, photographs are presented for only the measured condition. Longitudinal profiles are also included, to illustrate the bedforms that are the primary source of flow resistance in these stream types (David and others 2011).

The velocity data were collected using tracers (salt or dye), though different methodologies were used to compute the travel time (peak v. harmonic). Additionally, some of the cross-sectional data used to calculate the flow resistance coefficients were less prolific than other included datasets. Both the tracer travel time and the cross section spacing inconsistency may be sources of error, but considering the qualitative nature of using photographs to help choose resistance coefficients, the impact of these varying methods are likely inconsequential to users of this guide.

An overview of each of the data collection and processing methodologies is provided. For additional information, please refer to the supporting references.

Fraser Experimental Forest, Southern Rocky Mountains, USA

Data from the Fraser Experimental Forest of Colorado were collected in East Saint Louis (ESL) Creek and Fool Creek (FC), in the upper Colorado River basin on reaches of cascade, step-pool, transitional, and plane-bed form (David and others 2010, Yochum and others 2012). Slopes ranged from 1.5 to 20 percent, with channel reach lengths ranging from 6.2 to 31 m (21 to 101 ft) and widths from 1.1 to 4.0 m (3.5 to 13 ft). Reaches were initiated and terminated at similar bedform points and had consistent morphology, depth variability, and wood loading throughout. Instream wood was present, both within steps and dispersed throughout the reaches. Streamflow was dominated by snowmelt, with catchment areas from 0.69 to 8.7 km^2 (0.27 to 3.4 mi^2). Data collection consisted of longitudinal profiles at ~bankfull, medium, and low flows; bed, bank, and floodplain surveying; reach-average velocity measurements; bed-material characterization using pebble counts; and discharge measurements using V-notch weirs.

Reaches were surveyed during low flow using a terrestrial LiDAR scanner for above-water surface features and a gridded total station survey for below-water features. Cross sections were spaced at a uniform interval of 0.75 to 1.50 m (2.5 to 4.9 ft). At each resistance measurement, longitudinal profiles of the bed and water surface were measured at the thalweg and left and right edges of water. Bed particle size was measured using a 300-point pebble count. The slope of the water surface was assumed to be equivalent to S_f and was computed using the upstream and downstream water surface elevations divided by the longitudinal profile length.

Reach-average velocities were measured using a Rhodamine WT dye tracing methodology, using at least four replicate injections. Velocity was computed as the length of the thalweg longitudinal profile divided by the dye travel time. These data were collected with a 1 second time step. Travel time was computed using a spatial harmonic mean travel time (Walden 2004, Zimmermann 2010). To address data noise due to sunlight and aeration, a single-pass 3-point median smoothing methodology was applied (Tukey 1974, Gallagher and Wise 1981, Ataman and others 1981).

Rio Cordon, Alps, Italy

The Rio Cordon data were collected in the Dolomites of the Eastern Italian Alps (Comiti and others 2007), in a watershed with a catchment area of 5 km^2 (1.9 mi^2). The channels feature cascade and step-pool reaches, with little to no instream wood present as a consequence of the low forest cover (7% of the basin). Reach lengths varied from 16 to 41 m (53 to 133 ft), widths ranged from 3.8 to 5.8 m (12 to 19 ft), and slopes varied from 7.9 to 21 percent. Resistance was measured at a range of flows, from low to approximately 80% of the bankfull discharge. Discharge ranged from 0.17 to 1.86 m^3/s (6.0 to 66 ft^3/s). In contrast to the Fraser and Curran and Wohl (2003) reaches, the Rio Cordon reaches have less-developed bedforms. Using a total station, thalweg longitudinal profiles were surveyed and three cross-sections per reach were measured to characterize the channel geometry. These few sections were placed at intermediate locations between pools and steps, avoiding boulders and other irregularities. This method is a departure to the uniform-interval sections used in the other studies. Bed material size was measured using pebble counts of at least 100 clasts. Average velocity was measured using a salt tracer to measure travel time, which was computed using a difference in tracer peak concentrations. At least three injection replicates were performed per resistance measurement. The conductivity probes logged with an acquisition step of 5 seconds, which can potentially be a velocity error source in shorter reaches. Flow discharge was measured just downstream of the surveyed reaches, using weirs (Mao and others 2010).

Cascade Mountains, USA

The Cascade Mountains data were collected in streams both with (Curran and Wohl 2003) and without (MacFarlane and Wohl 2003) instream wood present, with this wood influencing the bed morphology and flow resistance. These data were collected in Washington State, at only low flow. The Curran and Wohl (2003) data consist of flow resistance measurements in reaches with slopes between 9.3 and 18 percent, lengths from 48 to 74 m (156 to 244 ft), flow widths from 1.7 to 3.2 m (5.6 to 10 ft), and beds composed of alluvium or a combination of alluvium and bedrock. Ten to 11 cross-sections were measured for each reach, with a spacing of roughly 5 meters. The MacFarlane and Wohl (2003) data consist of measurements in streams with slopes between 5.1 and 14 percent, lengths from 48 to 58 m (156 to 192 ft), flow widths from 0.94 to 2.6 m (3.1 to 8.7 ft), and beds composed of alluvium, a combination of alluvium and bedrock, or bedrock. Ten cross-sections were measured at equal intervals, with sections in both steps and pools. Thalweg longitudinal profiles were surveyed to measure the slope, quantify the bed profile, and provide the flow path lengths for the velocity computations. Discharge was not measured. Bed material size was measured using pebble counts. Average velocity was measured using a salt tracer to measure travel time, computed using a difference in tracer peak concentrations.

Araucania Region and Tierra del Fuego, Chile and Argentina

Data were collected in the Tres Arroyos watershed, in the Malalcahuello National Reserve in the Chilean Araucania region and in the Buena Esperanza basin, in the Argentine Tierra del Fuego near the city of Ushuaia (Comiti and others 2008). Catchment areas are 9.1 and 12.9 km^2 (3.5 to 5.0 mi^2) for Tres Arroyos and Buena Esperanza, respectively. The Comiti and others (2008) data was collected in channels with slopes between 2.2 and 15 percent, lengths from 17 to 99 m (57 to 324 ft), and flow widths from 2.8 to 5.3 m (9.1 to 17 ft). Longitudinal profiles were measured along the thalweg using a laser distance meter with inclinometer, and three cross sections per channel reach were surveyed using the same device. Field measurements of discharge and reach-averaged flow velocity were carried out using the salt tracer method. Portable conductivity meters were placed at the upstream and downstream ends of each study reach. A salt mixture (0.1 to 0.6 kg of salt dissolved in a plastic bucket) was injected into the main stream at a distance of at least 10 channel widths upstream from the upper probe, with the conductivity measured every 1 second. At least three replicate injections were performed. Reach-average velocity was derived from the thalweg length of the reach (from the longitudinal profile) and the time lag between the conductivity peaks. Water stage at the selected cross sections was measured just after each discharge and velocity measurement. Bed surface grain size distribution of each reach was characterized by a grid-by-number survey of at least 100 particles.

New Zealand

The New Zealand data (Wohl and Wilcox 2005) were collected on the South Island in the Southern Alps, in the Porter, Kowai, and Camp Creek watersheds on cascade, step-pool, plane-bed and transitional reaches with little to no instream wood present. Average annual precipitation varies substantially within the studied watersheds, from about 750 – 8000 mm (29 – 310 inches), from frontal systems and, very occasionally, dissipating tropical cyclones. Catchment areas range from 0.7 to 26 km^2 (0.27 to 9.9 mi^2). Reach lengths varied from 30 to 88 meters (98 to 287 ft), widths ranged from 1.6 to 29 m (5.2 to 96 ft), and slopes varied from 0.3 to 19 percent. The reaches were defined by lengths with consistent bed gradient and bedform type. Relevant data collection consisted of: (1) surveyed channel bed, water surface and high water mark (bankfull) gradients; (2) measured grain size, through pebble counts; and (3) average flow velocity using a salt tracer and conductivity probes. Hydraulic radius (R) values for these low flow measurements were estimated using approximate average flow depths, introducing uncertainty to these resistance estimates. Reach-average velocity was computed using the longitudinal profile length and the time lag between the conductivity peaks.

Flow Resistance Processes and Quantitative Prediction

Flow velocity and resistance coefficient estimates are required for numerous purposes, including hydraulic modeling, geomorphic and stream restoration analyses, and ecological assessments. Additionally, because small, steep channels in mountainous regions typically have very limited direct, systematic discharge records (Wohl 2010), indirect methods are often used to estimate discharge at the reach scale. Inaccurate estimation of a flow resistance coefficient will most likely produce inaccurate reach-average velocity and indirect discharge estimates, with numerous repercussions for hydrologic analyses and restoration designs. Hence, the selection of an appropriate Manning's n is very important.

Most methods for predicting velocity and discharge have been developed for lower-gradient streams, and the assumptions that are typically made regarding flow state when indirectly estimating discharge have led to much discussion of the appropriateness of these methods for mountain channels. For example, most indirect methods of discharge estimation – such as slope-area computations based on the Manning equation (Dalrymple and Benson 1967), step-backwater methods (O'Connor and Webb 1988), or a simplified slope-area method that does not require an estimate of Manning's roughness coefficient (Sauer and others 1985) – assume steady, uniform or gradually varied flow. However, floods along steep streams are typically unsteady, are rapidly varying, and may be debris-charged (Glancy and Williams 1994). Indirect discharge estimates can therefore be in error because of scour and fill, rapid changes in flow, substantial sediment transport, and flow transitions between subcritical and supercritical flow (Jarrett 1987, Sieben 1997).

Despite an increasing research emphasis on the hydraulics of steep streams, flow processes in mountain streams remain less understood than those of lower-gradient alluvial channels. Here we review the concept of resistance to flow and sources of this resistance in steep streams, with specific examples drawn from research from the Fraser Experimental Forest and Rio Cordon (Figures ESL-6 – RC-5). With some understanding of these processes we will also summarize the available quantitative methods for flow resistance prediction in these stream types.

Flow Resistance

Under conditions of steady, quasi-uniform, two-dimensional, and fully developed turbulent flow over a deformable channel bed, flow resistance is caused by (1) viscous and pressure drag on grains of the bed surface (*grain roughness*), (2) pressure drag on bed and bank undulations (*form roughness*), and (3) pressure and viscous drag on sediment in transport above the bed surface (Griffiths 1987). Additionally, *spill resistance* associated with hydraulic jumps and wave drag on elements protruding above the water surface (Figure RC-5) can be the dominant flow resistance mechanism in high-gradient channels (Curran and Wohl 2003, Comiti and others 2009, David and others 2011). Because vertical flow velocities vary from a maximum near the free-surface of the flow to zero at the wall and bed, shear forces are created and produce viscous energy dissipation, known as

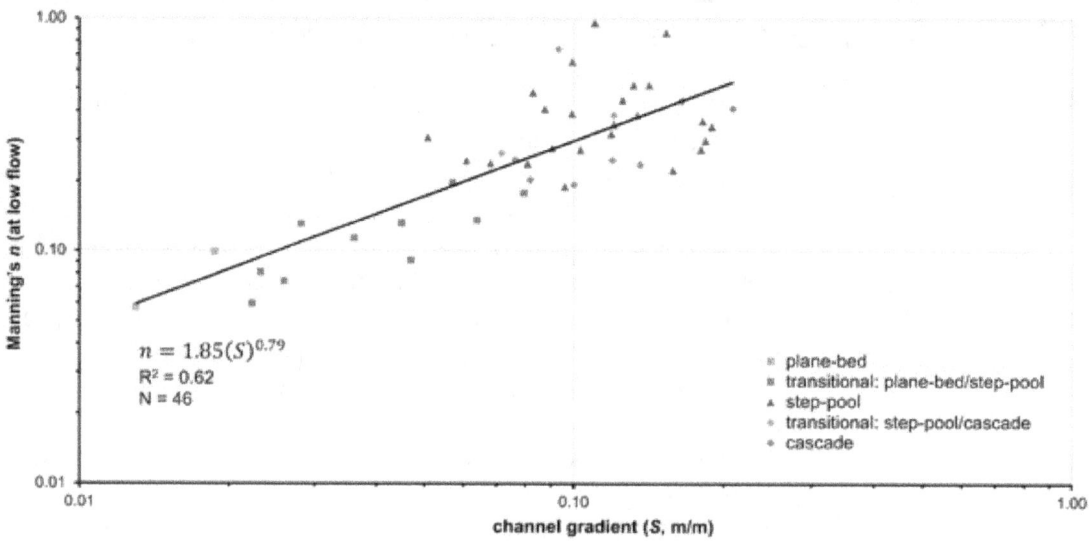

Figure 1: Manning's *n*, at low flow, versus channel gradient for the dataset presented in this report. Note the grouping of channel types as gradient increases.

skin friction (Tritton 1988). Form or pressure drag occurs because localized flow separation can create a high pressure upstream from an object and low pressure in the object's wake. The resulting pressure-gradient force opposes flow and creates viscous energy losses downstream from the object (Tritton 1988, Roberson and Crowe 1993).

The mechanisms producing flow resistance shift throughout a channel network, with transient bedforms such as dunes dominating flow resistance in low-gradient sand-bed channels, bed substrate and pool-riffle sequences creating most of the resistance in mid-gradient gravel-bed rivers, and boulder form drag (grain resistance) and spill resistance dominating high-gradient, stepped morphology (step-pool and cascade), boulder-bed channels (Bathurst 1993). All of these forms of energy dissipation are subsumed into a single resistance coefficient such as Manning's *n*. This flow resistance tends to increase as slope increases (Figure 1), with variation in flow resistance sources and dominant mechanisms, as well as flow stage, primarily contributing to the scatter.

Grain resistance represents the channel-bed roughness that induces energy losses resulting from skin friction and form drag from individual bed particles (Wiberg and Smith 1991). As depth increases, the individual particles influence a lower proportion of the flow and the effect of grain resistance is diminished (Wolman 1955). However, the coarse, poorly sorted clasts and relatively shallow flow of steep streams tend to make grain resistance more important in these channels than in most lower-gradient rivers, even during high flows. Consequently, grain roughness can dominate at high submergence, with form and spill roughness more important at low submergence (Parker and Peterson 1980, Hey 1988, Ferguson 2007, Zimmermann 2010).

The effect of flow depth relative to the height of individual sources of roughness is commonly expressed by R/D_c, where D_c is the roughness height. The roughness height is most commonly equated to the grain diameter for which x% is finer.

R/D_c is thus commonly expressed as R/D_{84}, known as *relative grain submergence*. Flow can be subdivided into large-scale roughness ($0 < R/D_{84} < 1$), intermediate-scale roughness ($1 < R/D_{84} < 4$), and small-scale roughness ($R/D_{84} > 4$) (Bathurst 1985; Ugarte and Madrid 1994), with shifts in velocity distributions and hydraulic resistance mechanisms as relative submergence decreases (Nikora and others 2001). The relative grain submergence ratio (alternatively expressed as h/D_{84}) is widely used – stemming from the Darcy-Weisbach flow resistance approach – to predict channel roughness in sand- and gravel-bed rivers (see Ferguson 2007), but it has been applied to step-pool streams as well (Lee and Ferguson 2002, Zimmermann 2010). However, the relative grain submergence does not account for bedforms (e.g., dunes, pool riffle, and step-pool sequences) or presence of step-forming instream wood. These bedforms can substantially increase channel roughness, from form and spill resistance. To account for this, the use of the standard deviation of bed profile (σ_z) has been advocated to better represent roughness height in channels with substantial bedforms (Aberle and Smart 2003, Coleman and others 2011, Yochum and others 2012).

A source of roughness in some mountain streams comes from instream wood. Individual pieces of wood can create grain or form resistance, depending on their size relative to adjacent bed topographic elements and flow depth (Wilcox and Wohl 2006). Logjams and wood steps substantially increase total flow resistance by altering bedform dimensions and, as a result, form and spill resistance (MacFarlane and Wohl 2003, Comiti and others 2008, David and others 2010, Wilcox and others 2011, Yochum and others 2012). Additional sources of flow resistance include bank roughness (Houjou and others 1990, Buffington 2012) and vegetation (Buffington and Montgomery 1999).

Examples of Flow Resistance Processes

To give more insight on flow resistance mechanisms, a practical illustration of flow resistance is provided for some of the photographic examples in this guide. First, brief discussions are presented on how resistance varies between reaches on the Rio Cordon and on East Saint Louis and Fool Creeks (Fraser Experimental Forest). Using the photographic guidance, more detailed descriptions are then presented on how flow resistance varies as flow changes for a subset of these reaches.

Rio Cordon

Measurements of flow resistance in the Rio Cordon were taken for a wide range of discharges, ranging from 0.17 to 1.86 m³/s (6.0 to 66 ft³/s; up to 80% of the bankfull discharge). The calculated Manning's n ranged from 0.12 to 0.41. Measurements taken at similar discharges show that flow resistance is higher in steeper and coarser reaches, where the bed becomes increasingly irregular and hydraulically rougher. For example, at lower flow (around 0.2 m³/s, 7 ft³/s), Manning's n is 0.41 in reach 5 (cascade, RC-5), 0.30 in reach 1b (step-pool, Figure RC-1b), and 0.18 in reach 1a (transitional from to plane-bed to step-pool, RC-1a). The presence of very coarse sediments, whether they are organized in steps or irregularly distributed creating a cascade morphology, is thus critical in increasing flow resistance.

In step-pool and cascade reaches, the spill component typically dominates over the other sources of resistance, mainly due to the tumbling flow generated by the presence of boulders or steps. Due to relatively poor development of pools and the virtual absence of large wood (Comiti and others 2007), flow resistance in step-pool and cascade reaches may be lower than in other high-gradient channels with similar slope. Comparison with the Fraser Experimental Forest data (Figures ESL-6 – FC-4 and Appendix A) illustrates this. As expected, flow resistance decreases with increasing discharge in all the study reaches at comparable rates, but the relative grain submergence ratio (R/D_{84}) was a poor predictor of flow resistance. No general thresholds (from nappe to skimming flows), similar to those observed in the laboratory by Comiti and others (2009), have been detected in the relationship between discharge and flow resistance. This is probably because the range of measured discharges did not exceed bankfull conditions and, with the main steps not fully submerged and spill resistance still dominant, a nappe flow regime was present in all the reaches. However, in a few reaches, reach-averaged Froude numbers approached unity.

In step-pool reach RC-1b, flow resistance was measured at a wider range of discharges, and flow velocities (and Froude numbers) varied considerably. The longitudinal profile shows three major steps (height about 1 m) with associated shallow pools downstream, and two smaller steps with almost no pool in the upstream part of the reach. The two large pools are asymmetrical and do not span the whole channel width. One of these steps is built around a mid-channel large boulder, whereas the upper large step is part of a mid-channel bar formed by coarse clasts lying unorganized on the bed. Upstream and downstream of these two steps, the bed is more symmetrical with lower channel-spanning steps. At the lower discharge (summer low flows, Q = 0.17 m^3/s = 6.0 ft^3/s), flow drops nearly vertically from the steps and dissipates all of the entire potential energy in the pools below. Even though these pools are quite shallow, they are still sufficient to contain the short and stable hydraulic jumps before the downstream steps. Jumps under these conditions are very effective in dissipating flow energy as the Froude number of the jet entering the pool is high (due to the large drop height relative to flow depth). The reach at such conditions features high flow resistance (n = 0.30). Flow resistance decreases to n = 0.24 as discharge increases to 0.9 m^3/s (31 ft^3/s) (Figure RC-1b-C), producing velocities that are sufficient to cause gravel transport (Lenzi and others, 2006a, 2006b). At this stage, flow aeration is considerably higher and small lateral bars are flooded, but the mid-channel bar is still mostly exposed. All the steps are still unsubmerged, but their jumps are rougher, longer (comparable to pool length), and have reduced energy dissipation efficiency. However, up to this stage, reach-averaged Froude numbers are quite low (0.2 – 0.35). At the highest discharge measured, 1.6 m^3/s (57 ft^3/s) at 70-75% of bankfull flow, the mid-channel bar is nearly submerged and only a few boulders protrude from the water surface (Figure RC-1b-B). At this stage, the median grain size of the bed surface is mobilized (Lenzi and others 2006a, 2006b) and the flow appears turbid, very rough, and aerated. The water surface profile is still strongly affected by the three major steps and the mid-channel bar, which are not hydraulically submerged, whereas the smaller steps upstream are fully submerged. Hydraulic jumps are now unstable and, in part, oscillating, indicating little efficiency in dissipating flow energy even at the taller steps. These conditions (overall, still characterizing a nappe flow regime for the reach) result in high reach-average velocities (V = 1.6 m/s = 5.3 ft/s), and the Froude number reveals that the flow is approaching critical conditions at a reach-averaged scale (Fr = 0.92). Flow resistance drops to n = 0.12, less than half the resistance of low flow.

Fraser Experimental Forest

Measurements of flow resistance for 14 reaches in Fraser Experimental Forest of Colorado have been included in this guide: one plane-bed, 10 step-pool and transitional, and 3 cascade channels. Data were collected in East Saint Louis Creek, and lower and upper Fool Creek, providing data at three channel sizes. Manning's n ranged from 0.05 to 0.30 for near-bankfull, 0.08 to 0.40 for mid-flow, and 0.10 to 0.52 for low-flow conditions. All reaches contained instream wood, with 95% of the wood located in the steps. The reaches typically had a combination of boulder steps and steps with wood held in place by one large keystone boulder. Two reaches without any step-forming wood (Figures FC-1 and ESL-3) had lower measured flow resistance, with bankfull n values of 0.095 and 0.20, and low flow n values of 0.16 and 0.25, respectively. These flow resistance values are similar to those measured in a couple of the Rio Cordon reaches (Figures FC-1a and RC-2a), where there was no instream wood. Conversely, wood-enhanced steps tend to be wider and taller than boulder-only steps, with typically higher measured flow resistance.

Dominant flow resistance mechanisms vary by reach and discharge, with non-step wood resistance contributing a large proportion of the total resistance at high flows and a progressively smaller proportion as discharge decreased and logs were no longer submerged, with the spill resistance increasing progressively as discharge decreased (David and others 2011). Step-forming wood contributes substantially to both form and spill resistance, due to wood increasing the step heights.

We use examples from two sites to demonstrate the influence of non-step-forming wood (Figure ESL-2) and step-forming wood (Figure FC-4). Reach ESL-2 had a bankfull n of 0.20 and low-flow n of 0.39, and reach FC-4 had a bankfull n of 0.22 and low-flow n of 0.52.

During high flows (Figure ESL-2-D) more than 70% of the resistance in ESL-2 was due to non-step wood while this component decreased to less than 10% during low flow, with spill resistance becoming dominant. Conversely, in FC-4 wood was predominantly located in steps and spill resistance was dominant for the full range in flows (David and others 2011). In all 13 of the cascade and step pool reaches, grain resistance contributed a small proportion of the total flow resistance, providing a contribution of less than 10% (David and others 2011).

Different components of resistance can combine to increase flow resistance at low flows while reducing resistance at high flows, as illustrated by the ESL-2 measurements. This reach contains three steps: two boulder-wood and one boulder. The wood in this reach is all found in the steps, except for one log that is only submerged during higher flows. The channel is narrow in the upstream and downstream portions, but wider in the middle. Some bedrock is exposed in the upstream section of the channel, prior to the final step. The farthest downstream step (Figure ESL-2-A, -D and -E) is taller and wider than the other two steps. The channel behind this step is subsequently wider and has smaller grain size material (D_{84} = 18 mm, compared to D_{84} = 70 mm for the entire reach) that has settled out. In general, step-pool reaches have greater variability in grain size throughout the different sections of the reach (step, tread, pool) than cascading reaches (David and others 2011). In ESL-2, the differences in grain sizes were most drastic among the various sections of the reach. Both the large step and the variability in grain size reveal an interaction of processes – the large step in the downstream portion of the reach created a large backwater area, which allowed the deposition of finer material and greater difference in flow acceleration between low and high flows. Grain resistance and ponding are significant at low flows when the grains are more exposed and water is backed up behind the large wood step. These two components cause a large increase in resistance and reduction of velocity during low flow (David and others 2010b).

As flow increases, the grains quickly become submerged, causing a substantial reduction in flow resistance and an increase in velocity. The upper two steps are almost completely submerged at bankfull flow, leaving the downstream step as the only significant drop and source of spill resistance. The combination of the reduction of grain resistance on the step tread leading up to the most downstream boulder-wood step, and the reduction of spill resistance over the upper two steps, results in the substantial reduction in flow resistance and increase in velocity, although at bankfull flow the reach-averaged Froude number is still substantially less than unity (0.35) and reach-average velocity is only 0.53 m/s (1.7 ft/s). The interaction of processes is important, because the large wood step in the downstream portion of this channel created a wider channel with smaller grain size, which then results in a reduced resistance and higher velocity at bankfull flows. Almost all the grains are submerged at bankfull flows, greatly reducing the importance of grain sorting throughout the different sections of the reach. At bankfull flows the drop over the step and the wood in the step become the most important sources of resistance.

Quantitative Prediction

This technical report was developed to provide photographic guidance for flow resistance in high-gradient channels, which is valuable for calibrating the predictive skills of practitioners who need to estimate resistance in these highly variable stream types. However, quantitative prediction methodologies are also needed, to reduce subjective judgment and assist with defining resistance variability as discharge changes. Simple relationships of slope versus resistance coefficients (Figure 1, Montgomery and Buffington 1997) are initial steps for quantifying flow resistance, but more comprehensive methods are desired. Despite the channel complexity and resulting flow resistance variability, the finding that bedforms provide the greatest contribution to flow resistance in these stream types (Comiti and others 2009, David and others 2011) can be leveraged for developing quantitative prediction methodologies.

Using the Fraser dataset, a number of existing methodologies for estimating resistance were assessed (Yochum 2010, Yochum and others 2012) for their predictive capabilities in steep streams. The results indicated that many of the available methods for predicting Manning's n (Jarrett 1984, Rickenmann 1994, Rice and others 1998) were not effective for prediction throughout the range of reach conditions and discharges. However, a review of the available methods for predicting f that are potentially applicable for these stream types (Thompson and Campbell 1979, Bathurst 1985, Kaufmann 1987, Lee and Ferguson 2002, Aberle and Smart 2003, Comiti and others 2007, Kaufmann and others 2008) found that the Aberle and Smart (2003) approach was relatively accurate. This method was developed using flume data on self-formed steps and uses the relative submergence term $\overline{h}/\sigma_z$, where $\overline{h}$ is the average flow depth (m) and σ_z is the standard deviation of the residuals of a bed profile regression (m). However, a systematic bias with this relationship was evident, with the methodology consistently underpredicting flow resistance in the Fraser streams.

Drawing on this finding, Yochum and others (2012) combined the Fraser dataset with the dataset developed by MacFarlane and Wohl (2003) to develop prediction equations based on field data using relative bedform submergence h_m/σ_z, where h_m is the median thalweg flow depth as measured from a longitudinal profile or a substantial number of equally-spaced cross sections. This dataset consisted of primarily alluvial and mixed alluvial-bedrock channels. These regressions, along with their 95% prediction intervals, are provided (Figure 2). The standard deviation of a bed profile regression (σ_z) is computed through

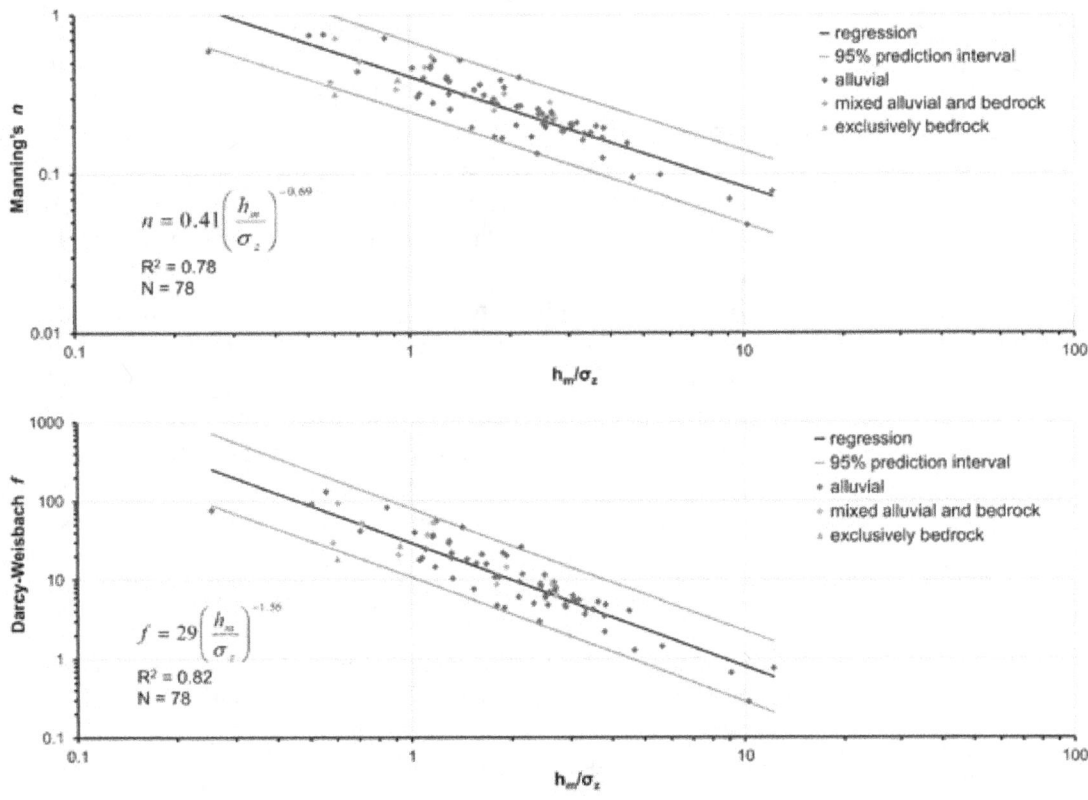

Figure 2: Regressions and 95% prediction intervals for Manning's n and Darcy-Weisbach f.

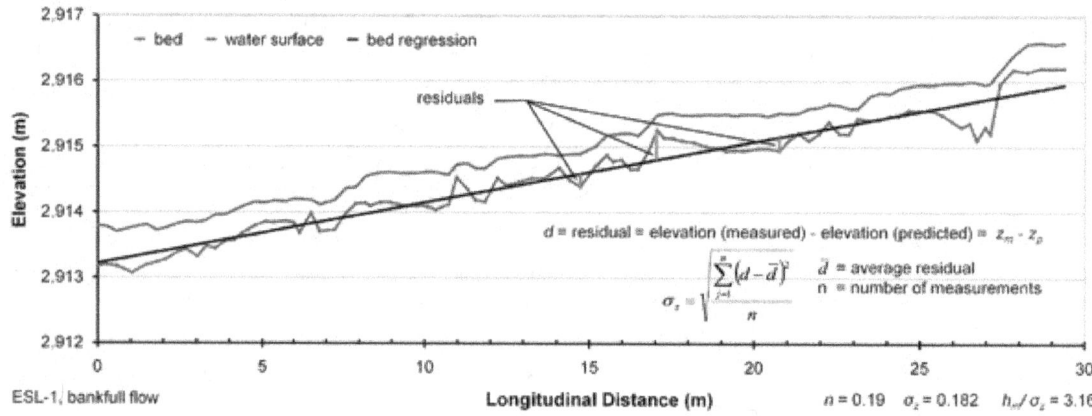

Figure 3: Computation methodology for σ_z.

measurement of a thalweg longitudinal profile – this computation is illustrated (Figure 3). For additional information on the method, refer to Yochum and others (2012).

These regression equations provide a method for quantitatively predicting flow resistance in high-gradient channels, for analysis and design purposes. However, limited data were available in their development and their applicability beyond the tested datasets is unknown. This may be especially problematic in larger channels; caution is warranted when extrapolating these results to channels of different scale, where other flow resistance mechanisms may be dominant.

Acknowledgments

Appreciation is expressed to the USDA Forest Service, the USDA Natural Resources Conservation Service, the National Science Foundation (EAR0608918), and the National Council for Air and Stream Improvement for project funding. The datasets and review provided by William MacFarlane and Janet Curran are greatly appreciated; their contributions to the single discharge measurements section provided substantial value to the report. Appreciation is expressed to the U.S. Forest Service Rocky Mountain Research Station for hosting the Fraser data collection, Tim Davies for facilitating field work in New Zealand, and Mario Lenzi for facilitating field work in Italy. Support from Dan Cenderelli and John Potyondy of the U.S. Forest Service Stream Systems Technology Center (STREAM TEAM) has been fundamental for the development of this report. Guidance on the execution of the research that forms the backbone of this work, from Brian Bledsoe, Sara Rathburn, and Chester Watson, has been highly valued. Appreciation is also expressed for the insightful comments by John Buffington and Sandra Ryan; their comments substantially increased the quality of the manuscript. Finally, field assistance by Mark Hussey, Dan Dolan, Andrew Wilcox, Lina Polvi, Bridget Diefenbach, Jason Alexander, Carla Brock, Paul Swartzinski, and Fred Wurster was fundamental for the development of these datasets.

References

Aberle, J., and G. M. Smart, 2003. The influence of roughness structure on flow resistance on steep slopes. *Journal of Hydraulic Research* 41(3): 259-269.

Aldridge, B. N., and J. M. Garrett, 1973. Roughness Coefficients for Stream Channels in Arizona. *U. S. Geological Survey Open-File Report*, Tucson, AZ.

Arcement, G. J., and V. R. Schneider, 1989. Guide for selecting Manning's roughness coefficients for natural channels and flood plains. *U. S. Geological Survey Water-Supply Paper 2339*.

Ataman, E., V. K. Aatre, and K. M. Wong, 1981. Some statistical properties of median filters. *IEEE Transactions on Acoustics, Speech, and Signal Processing* 29(5): 1073-1075.

Barnes, H. H., 1967. Roughness characteristics of natural channels. *U. S. Geological Survey Water-Supply Paper 1849*.

Bathurst, J. C., 1985. Flow resistance estimation in mountain rivers. *ASCE Journal of Hydraulic Engineering* 111: 625-641.

Bathurst, J. C., 1993. Flow resistance through the channel network. In: *Channel Network Hydrology*, Beven, K., and M. J. Kirkby (Eds.). John Wiley and Sons, Chichester, UK. pp. 69-98.

Buffington, J. M., 2012. Changes in channel morphology over human time scales. In: *Gravel-Bed Rivers: Processes, Tools, Environments*, Church, M., P. M. Biron, and A. G. Roy (Eds.). John Wiley and Sons, Chichester, UK, pp. 435-463.

Buffington, J. M., and D. R. Montgomery, 1999. Effects of hydraulic roughness on surface textures of gravel-bed rivers. *Water Resources Research* 35(11): 3507-3522.

Coleman, S. E., V. I. Nikora, and J. Aberle, 2011. Interpretation of alluvial beds through bed-elevation distribution moments. *Water Resources Research* 47: W11505.

Comiti, F., A. Andreoli, L. Mao, and M. A. Lenzi, 2008. Wood storage in three mountain streams of the Southern Andes and its hydro-morphological effects. *Earth Surface Processes and Landforms* 33: 244-262.

Comiti, F., D. Cadol, and E. Wohl, 2009. Flow regimes, bed morphology, and flow resistance in self-formed step-pool channels. *Water Resources Research* 45: doi:10.1029/2008WR007259.

Comiti, F., L. Mao, A. Wilcox, E. E. Wohl, and M. A. Lenzi, 2007. Field-derived relationships for flow velocity and resistance in high-gradient streams, *Journal of Hydrology* 340: 48–62.

Coon, W. F., 1998. Estimation of roughness coefficients for natural stream channels with vegetated banks. *U.S. Geological Survey Water-Supply Paper 2441*. 133 pp.

Curran, J. H. and E. E. Wohl, 2003. Large woody debris and flow resistance in step-pool channels, Cascade Range, Washington. *Geomorphology* 51(1-3): 141–157.

Dalrymple T, and M. A. Benson, 1967. *Measurement of peak discharge by the slope-area method.* Techniques of Water-Resources Investigations, U.S. Geological Survey, Book 3, Chapter A2. 12 pp.

Darcy, H. 1854. Sur des recherches expérimentales relatives au movement des eaux dans les tuyaux. *Comptes Rendus des Séances de l'Academie des Sciences* 38(11): 1109-1121.

David, G. C. L., 2011. *Characterizing flow resistance in steep mountain streams, Fraser Experimental Forest, CO.* PhD Dissertation, Colorado State University, Fort Collins, CO.

David, G. C. L., E. Wohl, S. E. Yochum, and B.P. Bledsoe, 2010a. Controls on at-a-station hydraulic geometry of steep mountain streams. *Earth Surface Processes and Landforms* 35: 1820–1837, doi:10.1002/esp.2023.

David, G. C. L., E. Wohl, S. E. Yochum, and B. P. Bledsoe, 2010b. Controls on spatial variations in flow resistance along steep mountain streams. *Water Resources Research* 46: W03513, doi:10.1029/2009WR008134.

David, G.C.L., E. Wohl, S.E. Yochum, B.P. Bledsoe, 2011. Comparative analysis of bed resistance partitioning in high-gradient streams. *Water Resources Research* 47: W07507, doi:10.1029/2010WR009540.

Ferguson, R., 2010. Time to abandon the Manning equation? *Earth Surface Processes and Landforms* 35: 1873-1876.

Ferguson, R. I. 2007. Flow resistance equations for gravel- and boulder-bed streams. *Water Resources Research* 43: W05427.

Gallagher, N. C., and G. L. Wise, 1981. A theoretical analysis of the properties of median filters. *IEEE Transactions on Acoustics, Speech, and Signal Processing* 29(6): 1136–1141.

Glancy, P. A., and R. P. Williams, 1994. Problems with indirect determinations of peak streamflows in steep, desert stream channels. In: *Hydraulic Engineering'94*, Cotroneo, G.V., and R.R. Rumer (Eds.). Proceedings of the 1994 National Conference of the Hydraulics Division, ASCE, New York. pp. 635-639.

Griffith, G. A., 1987. Form resistance in gravel channels with mobile beds. *ASCE Journal of Hydraulic Engineering* 115: 340-355.

Houjou, K., Y. Shimizu, and C. Ishii, 1990. Calculation of boundary shear stress in open channel flow. *Journal of Hydroscience and Hydraulic Engineering* 8(2): 21-37.

Hey, R. D., 1988. Bar form resistance in gravel-bed rivers. *ASCE Journal Hydraulic Engineering* 114: 1498-1508.

Hicks, D. M., and P. D. Mason, 1998. *Roughness Characteristics of New Zealand Rivers*, 2nd Edition, Water Resource Publications.

Jarrett, R. D., 1984. Hydraulics of high-gradient streams. *Journal of Hydraulic Engineering* 110 (11): 1519–1539.

Jarrett, R. D. 1987. Errors in slope-area computations of peak discharges in mountain streams. *Journal Hydrology* 96: 53-67.

Julien, P. Y., 1995. *Erosion and Sedimentation.* Cambridge University Press, NY. 280 pp.

Kaufmann, P. R., 1987. *Channel Morphology and Hydraulic Characteristics of Torrent-Impacted Forest Streams in the Oregon Coast Range, USA.* PhD Dissertation, Oregon State University, Corvallis, OR.

Kaufmann, P. R., J. M. Faustini, D. P. Larsen, and M. A. Shirazi, 2008. A roughness corrected index of relative bed stability for regional stream surveys. *Geomorphology* 99: 150–170.

Lee, A. J., and R. I. Ferguson, 2002. Velocity and flow resistance in step-pool streams. *Geomorphology* 46: 59–71.

Lenzi M. A., L. Mao, and F. Comiti. 2006a. Effective discharge for sediment transport in a mountain river: Computational approaches and geomorphic effectiveness. *Journal of Hydrology* 326: 257-276.

Lenzi M. A., L. Mao, and F. Comiti. 2006b. When does bedload transport begin in steep boulder-bed streams? *Hydrological Processes* 20: 3517-3533.

MacFarlane, W. A., and E. Wohl, 2003. Influence of step composition on step geometry and flow resistance in step-pool streams of the Washington Cascades. *Water Resources Research* 39(2): 1037.

Manning, R. 1891. On the flow of water in open channels and pipes. *Transactions of the Institution of Civil Engineers of Ireland* 20: 161-207.

Mao L., F. Comiti, and M. A. Lenzi, 2010. Bedload dynamics in steep mountain rivers: Insights from the Rio Cordon experimental station (Italian Alps). In: Gray, J.R., Laronne, J.B., and Marr, J.D.G., *Bedload-surrogate monitoring technologies.* Published online in 2010 as part of the U.S. Geological Survey Scientific Investigations Report 2010-5091: 253-265. Available only online: http://pubs.usgs.gov/sir/2010/5091/papers/Mao.pdf.

Montgomery, D. R., and J. M. Buffington, 1997. Channel reach morphology in mountain drainage basins. *Geological Society of America Bulletin* 109(5): 596–611.

Nikora, V., D. Goring, I. McEwan, and G. Griffiths, 2001. Spatially averaged open-channel flow over rough bed. *Journal of Hydraulic Engineering* 127 (2): 123–133.

O'Connor, J.E. and R.H. Webb, 1988. Hydraulic modeling for paleoflood analysis. In: *Flood geomorphology*, Baker, V.R., R.C. Kochel, and P.C. Patton, (Eds.). John Wiley and Sons, New York. pp. 393-402.

Parker, G. and A. W. Peterson. 1980. Bar resistance of gravel-bed streams. *ASCE Journal Hydraulics Division* 106: 1559-1575.

Phillips, J. V. and T. L. Ingersoll, 1998. Verification of roughness coefficients for selected natural and constructed stream channels in Arizona. *U.S. Geological Survey Professional Paper* 1584. 77 pp.

Reid, D. E. and E. J. Hickin, 2008. Flow resistance in steep mountain streams. *Earth Surface Processes Landforms* 33: 2211–2240.

Rice, C. E., K. C. Kadavy, and K. M. Robinson, 1998. Roughness of loose rock riprap on steep slopes. *Journal of Hydraulic Engineering* 124 (2): 179–185.

Rickenmann, D., 1994. An alternative equation for the mean velocity in gravel-bed rivers and mountain torrents. In: *Hydraulic Engineering '94*, Proceedings of the 1994 Conference, vol. 1. Cotroneo, G.V., and R.R. Rumer (Eds.). ASCE, Buffalo, NY. pp. 672-676.

Roberson J. A. and C. T. Crowe, 1993. *Engineering Fluid Mechanics.* John Wiley and Sons, New York. 823 pp.

Rosgen, D., 1996. *Applied River Morphology.* Wildland Hydrology, Pagosa Springs, CO.

Sauer V. B., R. E. Curtis, L. Santiago-Rivera, and R. Gonzalez, 1985. Quantifying flood discharges in mountainous tropical streams. In: *International Symposium on Tropical Hydrology and Second Caribbean Islands Water Resources Congress*, F. Quinones, and A.V. Sanchez (Eds.). American Water Resources Association, Bethesda, MD. pp. 104-108.

Sieben J., 1997. *Modeling of Hydraulics and Morphology in Mountain Rivers.* PhD dissertation, Technical University of Delft, The Netherlands. 223 pp.

Thompson, S. M., and S. M. Campbell, 1979. Hydraulics of a large channel paved with boulders. *Journal of Hydraulic Research* 17: 341–354.

Tritton D. J., 1988. *Physical Fluid Dynamics*. Clarendon Press, Oxford. 519 pp.

Tukey, J. W., 1974. Nonlinear (nonsuperposable) methods for smoothing data. *IEEE Electronics and Aerospace Systems Convention.* pp. 673.

Ugarte, A., and M. Madrid 1994. Roughness coefficient in mountain rivers. In: *Hydraulic Engineering '94*, Proceedings of the 1994 Conference, vol. 1. Cotroneo, G.V., and R.R. Rumer (Eds.). ASCE, Buffalo, NY. pp. 652-656,

Walden, M. G., 2004. Estimation of average stream velocity. *Journal of Hydraulic Engineering* 130(11): 1119–1122.

Weisbach, J., 1845. Lehrbuch der Ingenieur-und Mashchinenmechanik, Brunswick, Germany.

Wolman, M. G., 1955. The natural channel of Brandywine Creek Pennsylvania. *U.S. Geological Survey Professional Paper* 271. 56 pp.

Wiberg, P. L., and J. D. Smith, 1991. Velocity distribution and bed roughness in high-gradient streams. *Water Resources Research* 27(5): 825-838.

Wilcox A. C., and E. E. Wohl, 2006. Flow resistance dynamics in step-pool stream channels: 1. Large woody debris and controls on total resistance. *Water Resources Research* 42: W05418.

Wilcox A. C., E. E. Wohl, F. Comiti, and L. Mao, 2011. Hydraulics, morphology, and energy dissipation in an alpine step-pool channel. *Water Resources Research* 47: doi:10.1029/2010WR010192.

Wohl, E. E. 2010. *Mountain Rivers Revisited.* American Geophysical Union Water Resources Monograph 19, ISBN 978-0-87590-323-1.

Wohl, E. E., and Ikeda, H. 1998. The effect of roughness configuration on velocity profiles in an artificial channel. *Earth Surface Processes and Landforms* 23: 159-169.

Yochum, S. E., 2010. *Flow resistance prediction in high gradient streams.* PhD Dissertation, Colorado State University, Fort Collins, CO.

Yochum, S. E., B. P. Bledsoe, G. C. L. David, and E. Wohl, 2012. Velocity prediction in high-gradient channels. *Journal of Hydrology:* doi:10.1016/j. jhydrol.2011.12.031.

Zimmermann, A., 2010. Flow resistance in steep streams: An experimental study. *Water Resources Research* 46: W09536, doi:10.1029/2009WR007913

Photographic Guidance

Multiple Discharges

Nineteen figures are provided illustrating stream reach characteristics in plane-bed, step-pool (Figure 4), and cascade channels. Manning's n and Darcy-Weisbach f are provided for low, mid and high flows (Figures ESL-6 – RC-5). Photographs of the reaches from multiple perspectives and flow magnitudes are provided. Profile plots are also included, to depict the bed and water surface during bankfull flow. The photograph locations and orientations are shown as letters on the profile plots. The figures are ordered from lowest to highest average measured flow resistance.

Figure 4: Step-pool morphology in East Saint Louis Creek (ESL-1).

ESL-6 (plane-bed)

East Saint Louis Creek, Colorado, USA

S = 0.024 m/m; W = 3.0 m (9.8 ft); L = 6.4 m (21 ft)

7/12/2007
mid flow

low flow

mid flow
7/14/2008

8/13/2007

Fraser Experimental Forest;
Arapaho-Roosevelt National Forest
stream classification (Rosgen): B3

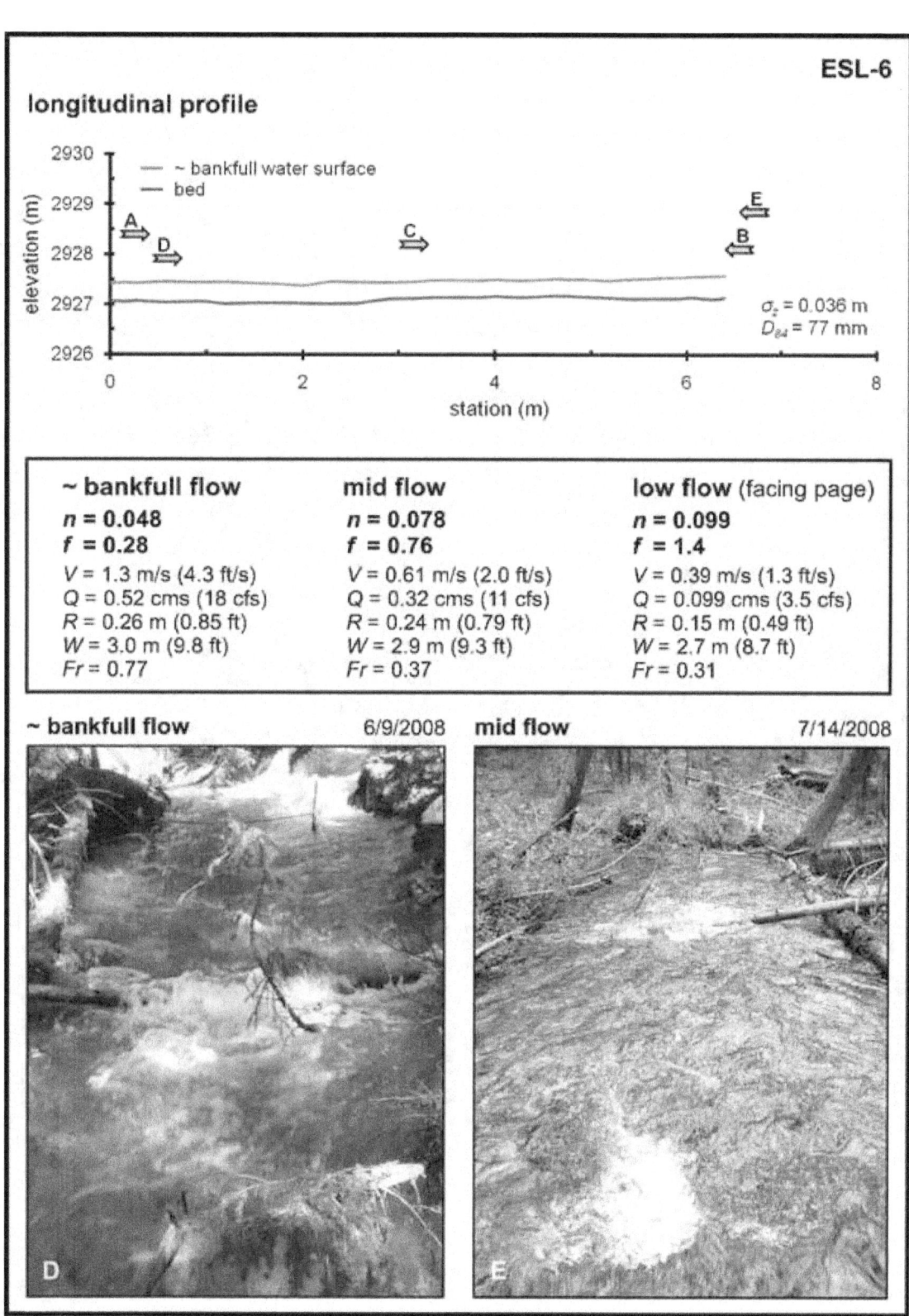

longitudinal profile

σ_z = 0.036 m
D_84 = 77 mm

$\sigma_z = 0.036$ m
$D_{84} = 77$ mm

~ bankfull flow	mid flow	low flow (facing page)
$n = 0.048$	$n = 0.078$	$n = 0.099$
$f = 0.28$	$f = 0.76$	$f = 1.4$
$V = 1.3$ m/s (4.3 ft/s)	$V = 0.61$ m/s (2.0 ft/s)	$V = 0.39$ m/s (1.3 ft/s)
$Q = 0.52$ cms (18 cfs)	$Q = 0.32$ cms (11 cfs)	$Q = 0.099$ cms (3.5 cfs)
$R = 0.26$ m (0.85 ft)	$R = 0.24$ m (0.79 ft)	$R = 0.15$ m (0.49 ft)
$W = 3.0$ m (9.8 ft)	$W = 2.9$ m (9.3 ft)	$W = 2.7$ m (8.7 ft)
$Fr = 0.77$	$Fr = 0.37$	$Fr = 0.31$

~ bankfull flow   6/9/2008

mid flow   7/14/2008

FC-1 (transitional: plane-bed / step-pool)

Fool Creek, Colorado, USA

S = 0.063 m/m; W = 2.0 m (6.5 ft); L = 23 m (76 ft)

low flow

9/25/2009

Fraser Experimental Forest;
Arapaho-Roosevelt National Forest

stream classification (Rosgen): A3

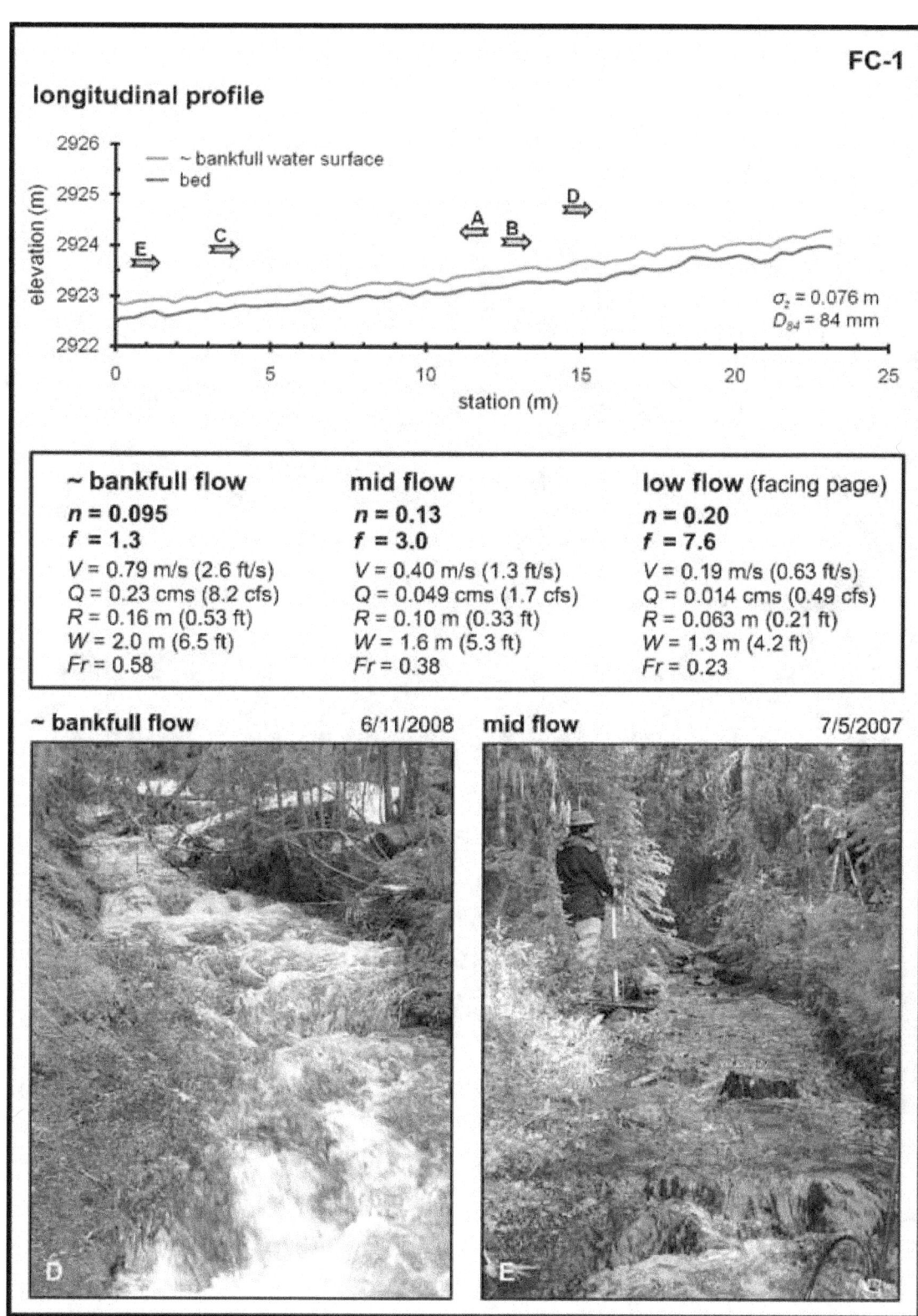

FC-1

longitudinal profile

~ bankfull water surface
bed

σ_z = 0.076 m
D_{84} = 84 mm

elevation (m)
station (m)

~ bankfull flow	**mid flow**	**low flow** (facing page)
n = 0.095	n = 0.13	n = 0.20
f = 1.3	f = 3.0	f = 7.6
V = 0.79 m/s (2.6 ft/s)	V = 0.40 m/s (1.3 ft/s)	V = 0.19 m/s (0.63 ft/s)
Q = 0.23 cms (8.2 cfs)	Q = 0.049 cms (1.7 cfs)	Q = 0.014 cms (0.49 cfs)
R = 0.16 m (0.53 ft)	R = 0.10 m (0.33 ft)	R = 0.063 m (0.21 ft)
W = 2.0 m (6.5 ft)	W = 1.6 m (5.3 ft)	W = 1.3 m (4.2 ft)
Fr = 0.58	Fr = 0.38	Fr = 0.23

~ bankfull flow 6/11/2008

mid flow 7/5/2007

RC-1a (transitional: plane-bed / step-pool)

Rio Cordon, Italy
S = 0.079 m/m; W = 4.8 m (16 ft); L = 23 m (75 ft)

low flow

7/29/2004

Dolomite range;
Eastern Italian Alps
stream classification (Rosgen): B3a

USDA Forest Service RMRS-GTR-323. 2014.

longitudinal profile

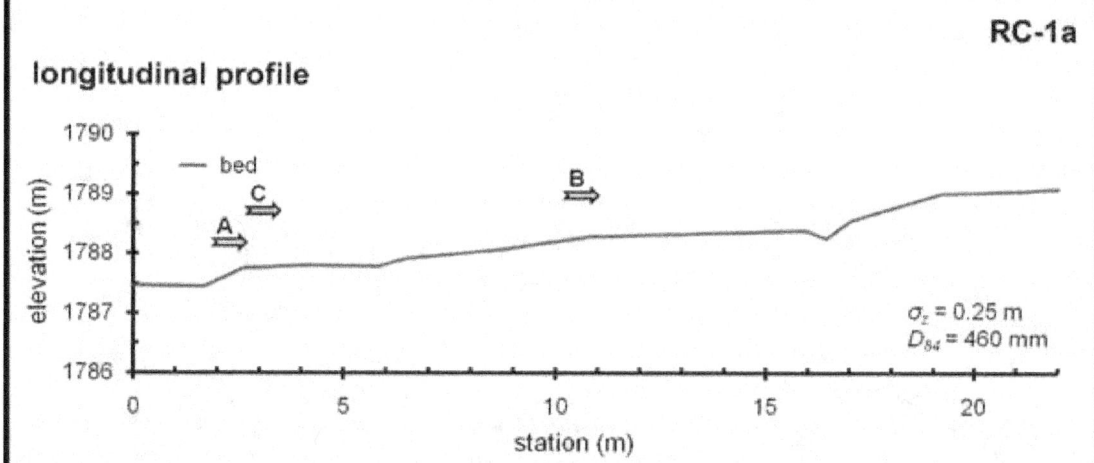

elevation (m)

— bed

$\sigma_z = 0.25$ m
$D_{84} = 460$ mm

station (m)

high flow	mid flow	low flow (facing page)
$n = 0.13$	$n = 0.18$	$n = 0.18$
$f = 1.8$	$f = 4.7$	$f = 5.0$
$V = 1.14$ m/s (3.7 ft/s)	$V = 0.48$ m/s (1.6 ft/s)	$V = 0.39$ m/s (1.3 ft/s)
$Q = 1.86$ cms (66 cfs)	$Q = 0.47$ cms (17 cfs)	$Q = 0.21$ cms (7.4 cfs)
$R = 0.38$ m (1.2 ft)	$R = 0.18$ m (0.60 ft)	$R = 0.12$ m (0.39 ft)
$W = 4.8$ m (16 ft)	$W = 4.2$ m (14 ft)	$W = 4.1$ m (14 ft)
$Fr = 0.63$	$Fr = 0.32$	$Fr = 0.35$

high flow   11/1/2004   **mid flow**   10/29/2004

RC-2a (step-pool)

Rio Cordon, Italy

S = 0.096 m/m; W = 5.7 m (19 ft); L = 29 m (96 ft)

low flow

7/29/2004

Dolomite range;
Eastern Italian Alps

stream classification (Rosgen): A3

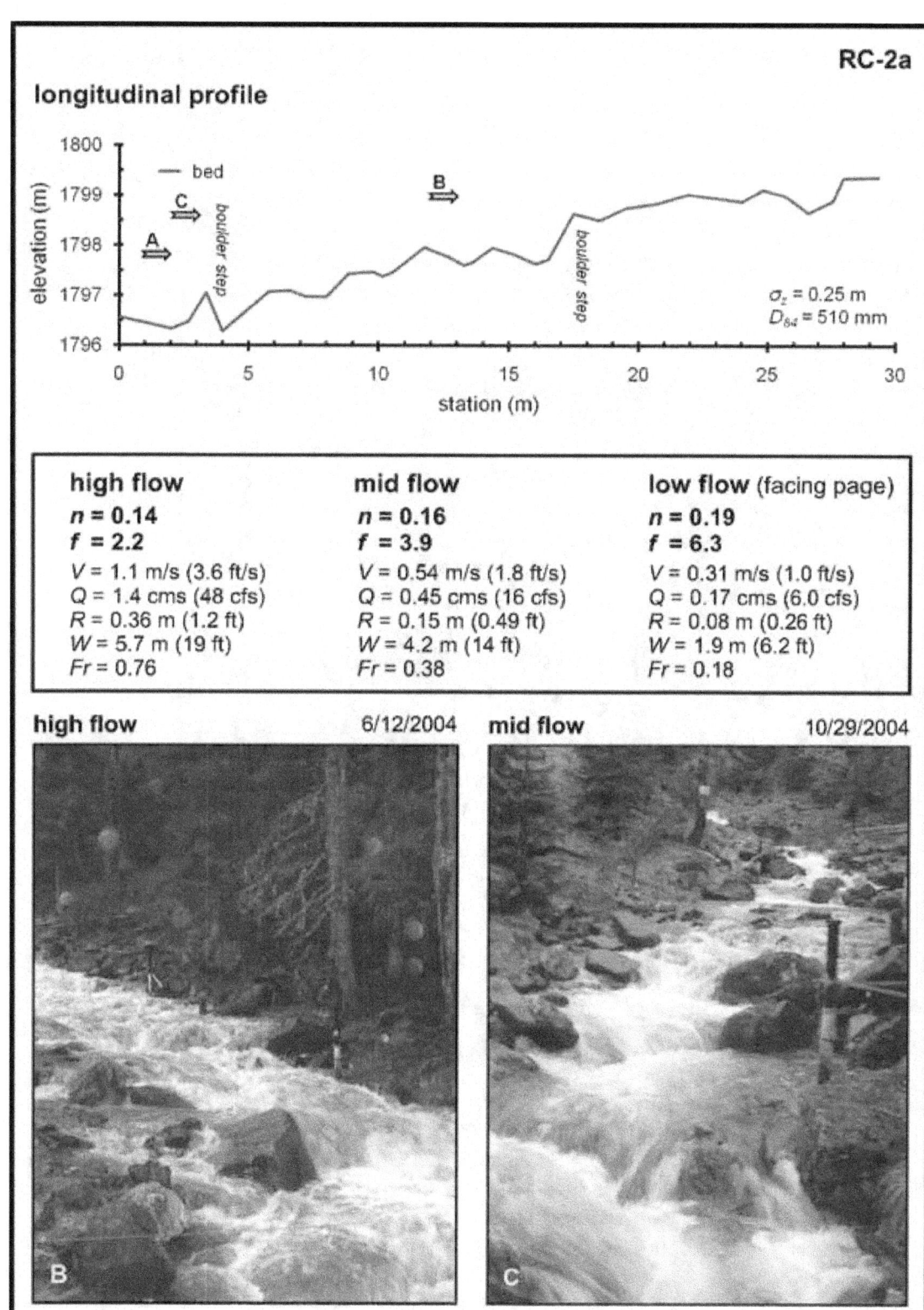

RC-2a

longitudinal profile

elevation (m) vs station (m)

— bed

σ_z = 0.25 m
D_{84} = 510 mm

boulder step

boulder step

high flow	**mid flow**	**low flow** (facing page)
n = 0.14	n = 0.16	n = 0.19
f = 2.2	f = 3.9	f = 6.3
V = 1.1 m/s (3.6 ft/s)	V = 0.54 m/s (1.8 ft/s)	V = 0.31 m/s (1.0 ft/s)
Q = 1.4 cms (48 cfs)	Q = 0.45 cms (16 cfs)	Q = 0.17 cms (6.0 cfs)
R = 0.36 m (1.2 ft)	R = 0.15 m (0.49 ft)	R = 0.08 m (0.26 ft)
W = 5.7 m (19 ft)	W = 4.2 m (14 ft)	W = 1.9 m (6.2 ft)
Fr = 0.76	Fr = 0.38	Fr = 0.18

high flow   6/12/2004

mid flow   10/29/2004

B

C

FC-2 (step-pool)

Fool Creek, Colorado, USA

S = 0.071 m/m; W = 1.6 m (5.3 ft); L = 14 m (47 ft)

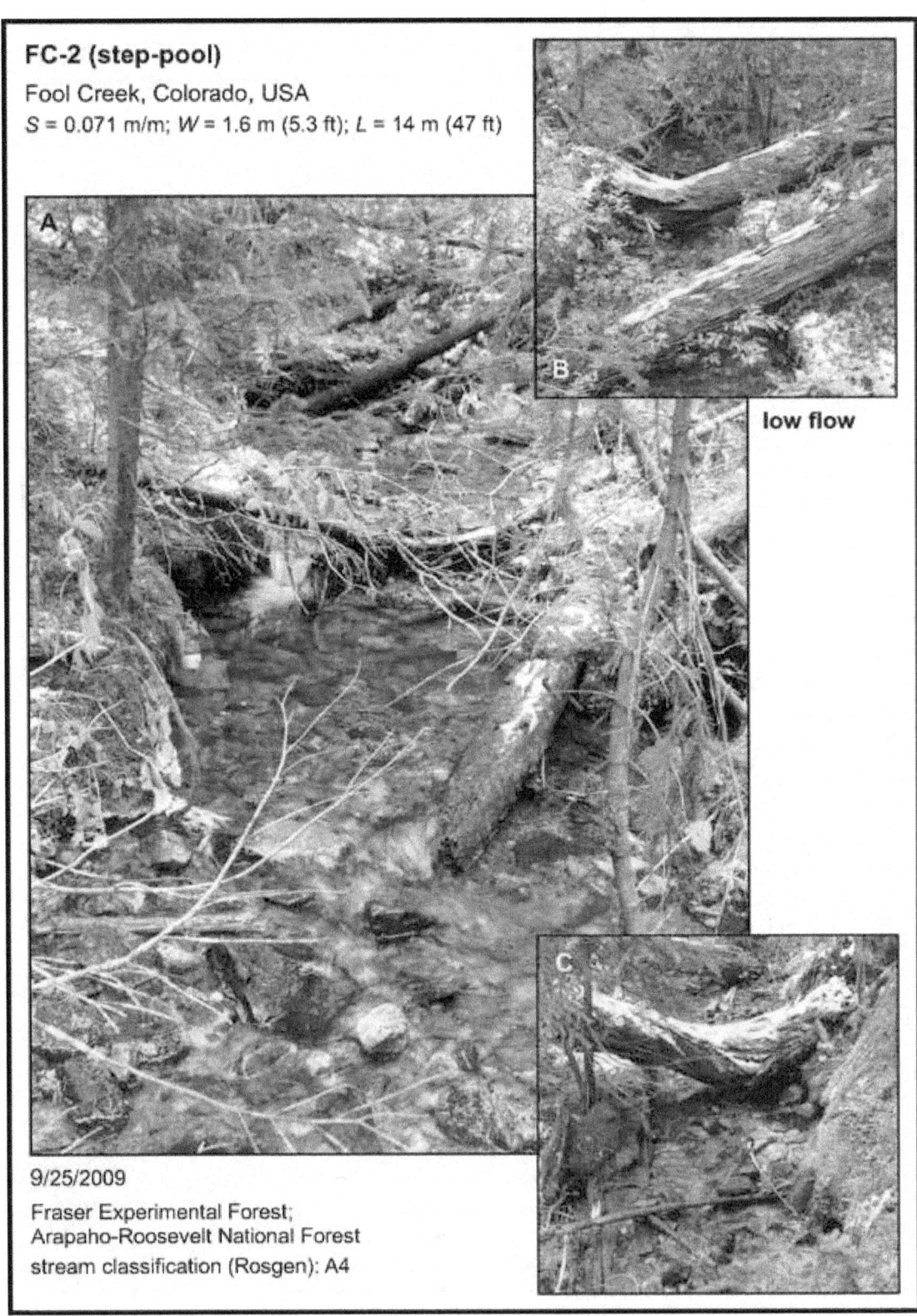

low flow

9/25/2009

Fraser Experimental Forest;
Arapaho-Roosevelt National Forest

stream classification (Rosgen): A4

FC-2

longitudinal profile

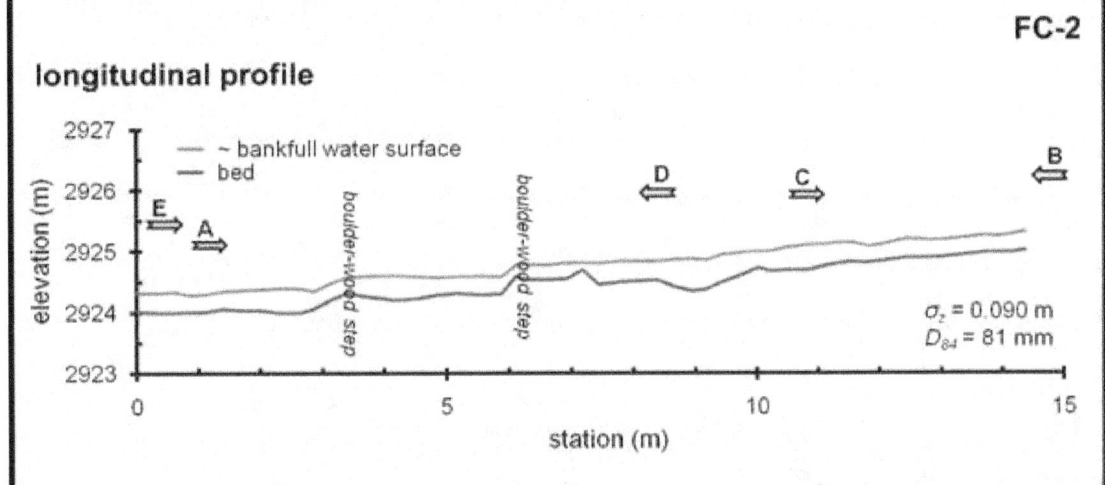

~ bankfull water surface
bed

$\sigma_z = 0.090$ m
$D_{84} = 81$ mm

boulder-wood step
boulder-wood step

~ bankfull flow	mid flow	low flow (facing page)
$n = 0.13$	$n = 0.22$	$n = 0.24$
$f = 2.2$	$f = 8.0$	$f = 11$
$V = 0.66$ m/s (2.2 ft/s)	$V = 0.28$ m/s (0.91 ft/s)	$V = 0.17$ m/s (0.55 ft/s)
$Q = 0.24$ cms (8.5 cfs)	$Q = 0.038$ cms (1.3 cfs)	$Q = 0.013$ cms (0.45 cfs)
$R = 0.18$ m (0.59 ft)	$R = 0.11$ m (0.36 ft)	$R = 0.060$ m (0.20 ft)
$W = 1.6$ m (6.5 ft)	$W = 1.4$ m (4.6 ft)	$W = 1.1$ m (3.7 ft)
$Fr = 0.44$	$Fr = 0.24$	$Fr = 0.21$

~ bankfull flow   6/13/2008

mid flow   7/23/2008

ESL-7 (cascade)

East Saint Louis Creek, Colorado, USA
S = 0.085 m/m; W = 3.0 m (10.0 ft); L = 22 m (72 ft)

low flow

9/25/2009

Fraser Experimental Forest;
Arapaho-Roosevelt National Forest

stream classification (Rosgen): B3a

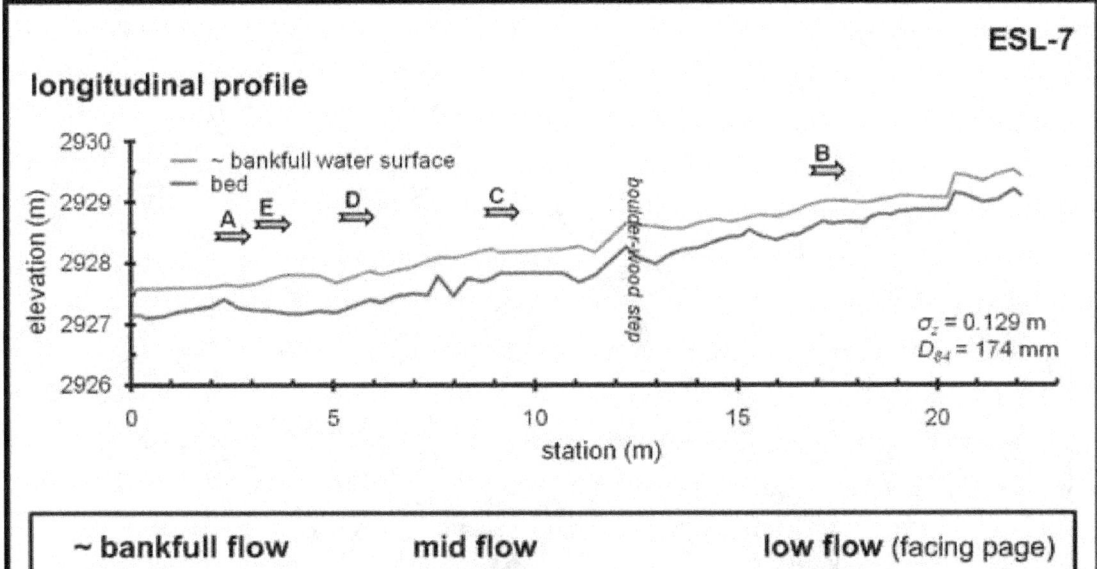

ESL-7

longitudinal profile

elevation (m) vs station (m)

~ bankfull water surface
bed

boulder-wood step

σ_z = 0.129 m
D_{84} = 174 mm

~ bankfull flow	mid flow	low flow (facing page)
n = 0.17	n = 0.19	n = 0.20
f = 3.5	f = 4.9	f = 6.0
V = 0.69 m/s (2.3 ft/s)	V = 0.55 m/s (1.8 ft/s)	V = 0.40 m/s (1.3 ft/s)
Q = 0.52 cms (18 cfs)	Q = 0.30 cms (11 cfs)	Q = 0.10 cms (3.6 cfs)
R = 0.25 m (0.83 ft)	R = 0.23 m (0.75 ft)	R = 0.15 m (0.49 ft)
W = 3.0 m (9.9 ft)	W = 2.9 m (9.6 ft)	W = 2.5 m (8.1 ft)
Fr = 0.39	Fr = 0.32	Fr = 0.31

~ bankfull flow 6/8/2008

mid flow 7/15/2008

ESL-3 (cascade)

East Saint Louis Creek, Colorado, USA
S = 0.13 m/m; W = 3.6 m (12 ft); L = 10 m (34 ft)

low flow

9/26/2009

Fraser Experimental Forest;
Arapaho-Roosevelt National Forest
stream classification (Rosgen): B3a

longitudinal profile

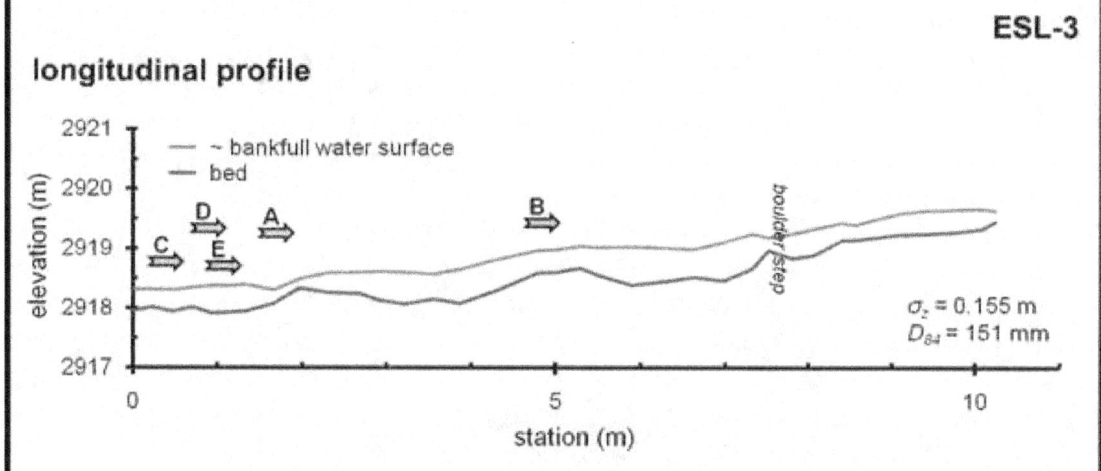

$\sigma_z = 0.155$ m
$D_{84} = 151$ mm

~ bankfull flow	mid flow	low flow (facing page)
$n = 0.16$	$n = 0.20$	$n = 0.25$
$f = 3.7$	$f = 5.7$	$f = 9.2$
$V = 0.71$ m/s (2.3 ft/s)	$V = 0.54$ m/s (1.8 ft/s)	$V = 0.38$ m/s (1.2 ft/s)
$Q = 0.46$ cms (16 cfs)	$Q = 0.30$ cms (11 cfs)	$Q = 0.089$ cms (3.1 cfs)
$R = 0.18$ m (0.60 ft)	$R = 0.17$ m (0.57 ft)	$R = 0.14$ m (0.46 ft)
$W = 3.6$ m (12 ft)	$W = 3.5$ m (12 ft)	$W = 2.4$ m (7.9 ft)
$Fr = 0.46$	$Fr = 0.36$	$Fr = 0.29$

~ bankfull flow   6/7/2008

mid flow   7/15/2008

ESL-8 (step-pool)

East Saint Louis Creek, Colorado, USA

S = 0.094 m/m; W = 3.2 m (10.4 ft); L = 31 m (101 ft)

low flow

9/25/2009

Fraser Experimental Forest;
Arapaho-Roosevelt National Forest
stream classification (Rosgen): A3

longitudinal profile

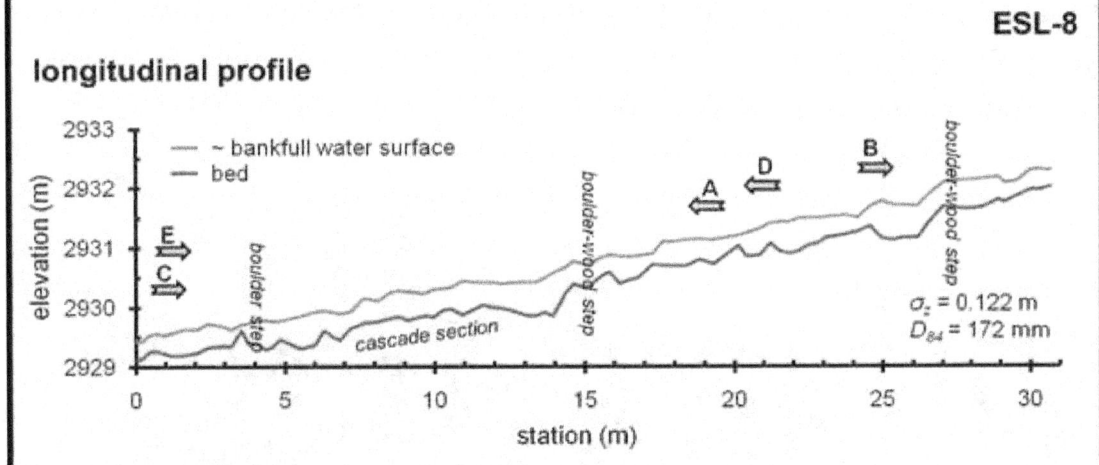

ESL-8

elevation (m)

~ bankfull water surface
bed

$\sigma_z = 0.122$ m
$D_{84} = 172$ mm

boulder step
cascade section
boulder-wood step
boulder-wood step

station (m)

~ **bankfull flow**	**mid flow**	**low flow** (facing page)
$n = 0.18$	$n = 0.20$	$n = 0.24$
$f = 4.2$	$f = 5.3$	$f = 8.2$
$V = 0.64$ m/s (2.1 ft/s)	$V = 0.53$ m/s (1.7 ft/s)	$V = 0.35$ m/s (1.2 ft/s)
$Q = 0.46$ cms (16 cfs)	$Q = 0.29$ cms (10 cfs)	$Q = 0.10$ cms (3.5 cfs)
$R = 0.23$ m (0.76 ft)	$R = 0.21$ m (0.70 ft)	$R = 0.16$ m (0.52 ft)
$W = 3.2$ m (10.4 ft)	$W = 3.0$ m (9.9 ft)	$W = 2.6$ m (8.5 ft)
$Fr = 0.38$	$Fr = 0.33$	$Fr = 0.26$

~ bankfull flow   6/9/2008   7/16/2008

RC-1b (step-pool)

Rio Cordon, Italy

S = 0.18 m/m; W = 5.4 m (18 ft); L = 16 m (53 ft)

low flow

7/29/2004

Dolomite range;
Eastern Italian Alps

stream classification (Rosgen): A3a+

RC-1b

longitudinal profile

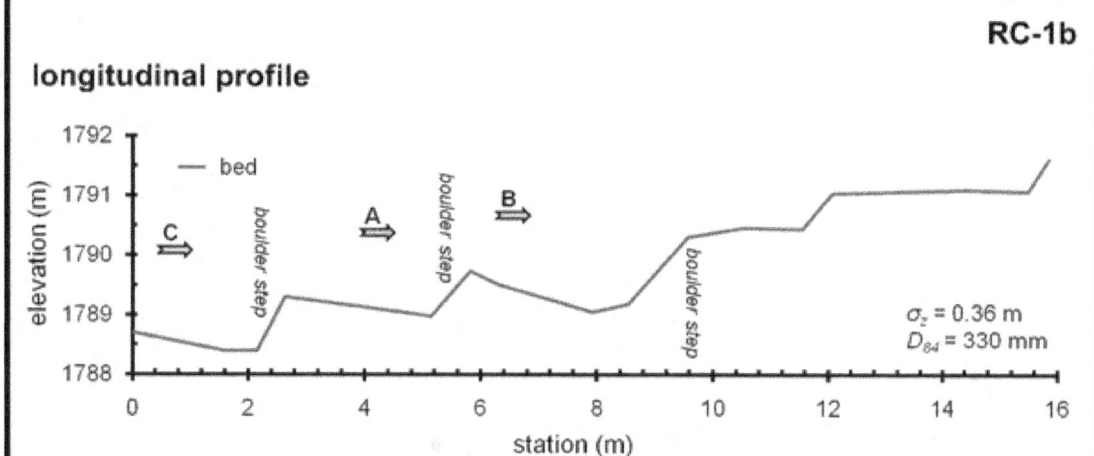

σ_z = 0.36 m
D_{84} = 330 mm

high flow	**mid flow**	**low flow** (facing page)
n = 0.12	n = 0.24	n = 0.30
f = 1.6	f = 7.4	f = 16
V = 1.6 m/s (5.3 ft/s)	V = 0.64 m/s (2.1 ft/s)	V = 0.28 m/s (0.92 ft/s)
Q = 1.6 cms (57 cfs)	Q = 0.89 cms (31 cfs)	Q = 0.17 cms (6.0 cfs)
R = 0.28 m (0.92 ft)	R = 0.21 m (0.69 ft)	R = 0.090 m (0.30 ft)
W = 5.4 m (18 ft)	W = 3.8 m (13 ft)	W = 2.9 m (9.5 ft)
Fr = 0.92	Fr = 0.34	Fr = 0.20

high flow   11/1/2004   **mid flow**   5/25/2004

ESL-1 (step-pool)

East Saint Louis Creek, Colorado, USA
S = 0.096 m/m; W = 2.9 m (9.6 ft); L = 29 m (96 ft)

low flow

9/26/2009

Fraser Experimental Forest;
Arapaho-Roosevelt National Forest
stream classification (Rosgen): B3a

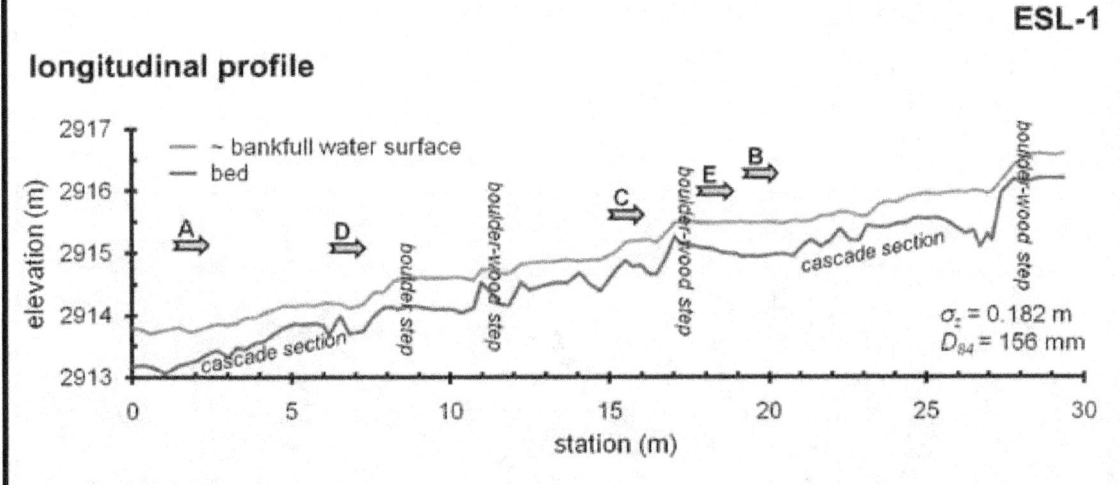

ESL-1

longitudinal profile

elevation (m) vs *station (m)*

— ~ bankfull water surface
— bed

A D C E B

cascade section boulder step boulder-wood step boulder-wood step cascade section boulder-wood step

$\sigma_z = 0.182$ m
$D_{84} = 156$ mm

~ bankfull flow	mid flow
$n = 0.19$	$n = 0.27$
$f = 4.5$	$f = 9.4$
$V = 0.65$ m/s (2.1 ft/s)	$V = 0.42$ m/s (1.4 ft/s)
$Q = 0.60$ cms (20 cfs)	$Q = 0.24$ cms (8.3 cfs)
$R = 0.25$ m (0.83 ft)	$R = 0.20$ m (0.67 ft)
$W = 2.9$ m (9.6 ft)	$W = 2.6$ m (8.5 ft)
$Fr = 0.35$	$Fr = 0.26$

~ bankfull flow   6/10/2008

mid flow   7/22/2008

RC-3 (cascade)

Rio Cordon, Italy

S = 0.14 m/m; W = 3.8 m (12 ft); L = 38 m (125 ft)

low flow

7/29/2004

Dolomite range;
Eastern Italian Alps
stream classification (Rosgen): A3a+

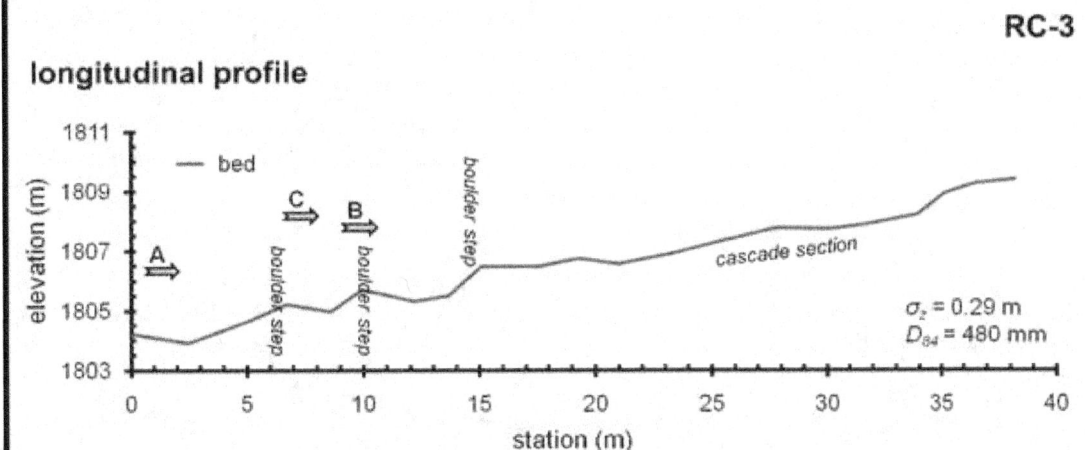

RC-3

longitudinal profile

(graph: elevation (m) vs station (m); "bed" curve; labels A, B, C with arrows; boulder step, boulder step, boulder step; cascade section; $\sigma_z = 0.29$ m, $D_{84} = 480$ mm)

high flow	**mid flow**	**low flow** (facing page)
$n = 0.20$	$n = 0.24$	$n = 0.24$
$f = 4.5$	$f = 8.3$	$f = 8.9$
$V = 0.86$ m/s (2.8 ft/s)	$V = 0.5$ m/s (1.6 ft/s)	$V = 0.37$ m/s (1.2 ft/s)
$Q = 0.93$ cms (33 cfs)	$Q = 0.47$ cms (17 cfs)	$Q = 0.21$ cms (7.4 cfs)
$R = 0.31$ m (1.01 ft)	$R = 0.2$ m (0.66 ft)	$R = 0.12$ m (0.39 ft)
$W = 3.8$ m (12 ft)	$W = 3.5$ m (11 ft)	$W = 3.3$ m (11 ft)
$Fr = 0.51$	$Fr = 0.31$	$Fr = 0.29$

high flow　　　11/1/2004　　　**mid flow**　　　6/24/2004

ESL-9 (step-pool)

East Saint Louis Creek, Colorado, USA
S = 0.11 m/m; W = 2.8 m (9.2 ft); L = 16 m (53 ft)

low flow

9/26/2009

Fraser Experimental Forest;
Arapaho-Roosevelt National Forest
stream classification (Rosgen): B3a

44

longitudinal profile

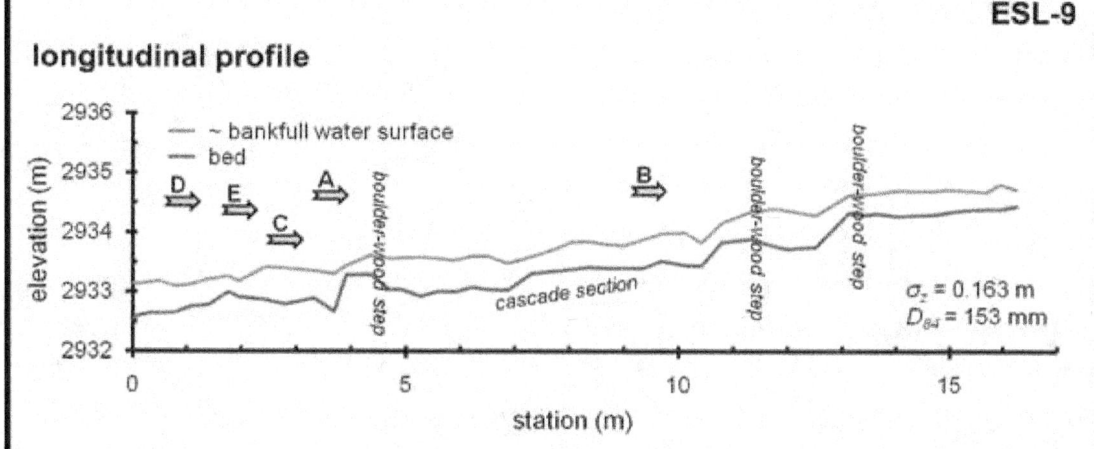

~ bankfull water surface
bed

D
E
C
A
B

boulder-wood step
cascade section
boulder-wood step
boulder-wood step

σ_z = 0.163 m
D_{84} = 153 mm

elevation (m)

station (m)

~ bankfull flow	mid flow	low flow (facing page)
n = 0.21	n = 0.26	n = 0.28
f = 5.5	f = 8.8	f = 10.9
V = 0.64 m/s (2.1 ft/s)	V = 0.43 m/s (1.4 ft/s)	V = 0.33 m/s (1.1 ft/s)
Q = 0.57 cms (20 cfs)	Q = 0.20 cms (7.1 cfs)	Q = 0.11 cms (3.8 cfs)
R = 0.25 m (0.82 ft)	R = 0.20 m (0.66 ft)	R = 0.17 m (0.55 ft)
W = 2.8 m (9.2 ft)	W = 2.6 m (8.5 ft)	W = 2.3 m (7.5 ft)
Fr = 0.36	Fr = 0.27	Fr = 0.23

~ bankfull flow   6/8/2008

D

mid flow   7/11/2007

E

ESL-2 (step-pool)

East Saint Louis Creek, Colorado, USA
S = 0.094 m/m; W = 3.2 m (11 ft); L = 14 m (45 ft)

low flow

9/26/2009

Fraser Experimental Forest;
Arapaho-Roosevelt National Forest
stream classification (Rosgen): B3a

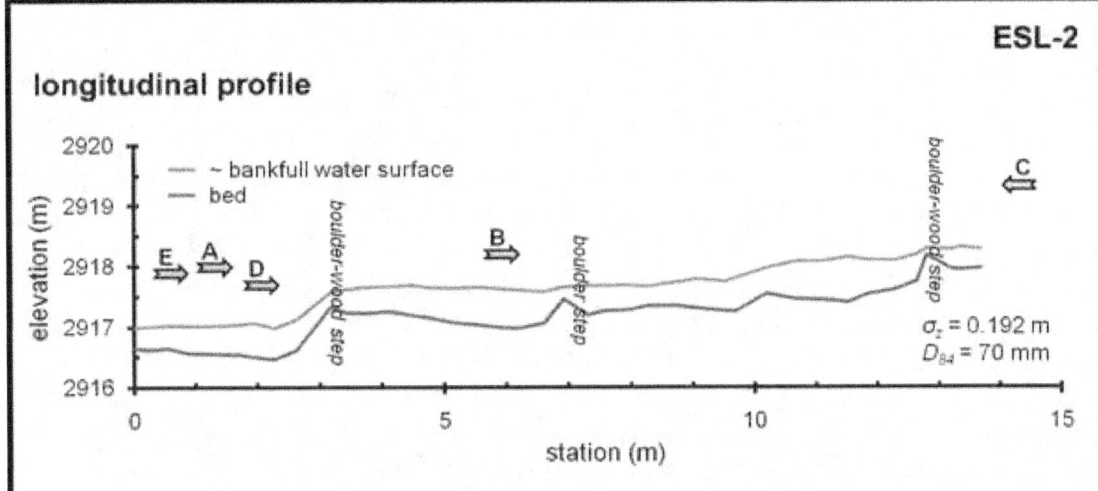

ESL-2

longitudinal profile

- ~ bankfull water surface
- bed

$\sigma_z = 0.192$ m
$D_{84} = 70$ mm

boulder-wood step

boulder step

boulder-wood step

~ bankfull flow
$n = 0.20$
$f = 4.8$
$V = 0.61$ m/s (2.0 ft/s)
$Q = 0.53$ cms (18 cfs)
$R = 0.25$ m (0.81 ft)
$W = 3.2$ m (11 ft)
$Fr = 0.35$

mid flow
$n = 0.23$
$f = 7.0$
$V = 0.45$ m/s (1.5 ft/s)
$Q = 0.22$ cms (7.7 cfs)
$R = 0.20$ m (0.65 ft)
$W = 2.9$ m (9.4 ft)
$Fr = 0.30$

low flow (facing page)
$n = 0.39$
$f = 22$
$V = 0.24$ m/s (0.77 ft/s)
$Q = 0.094$ cms (3.3 cfs)
$R = 0.16$ m (0.51 ft)
$W = 2.6$ m (8.4 ft)
$Fr = 0.18$

~ bankfull flow   6/6/2008

D

mid flow   7/9/2007

E

ESL-4 (step-pool)

East Saint Louis Creek, Colorado, USA
S = 0.12 m/m; W = 2.9 m (9.4 ft); L = 16 m (51 ft)

low flow

9/26/2009

Fraser Experimental Forest;
Arapaho-Roosevelt National Forest
stream classification (Rosgen): B3a

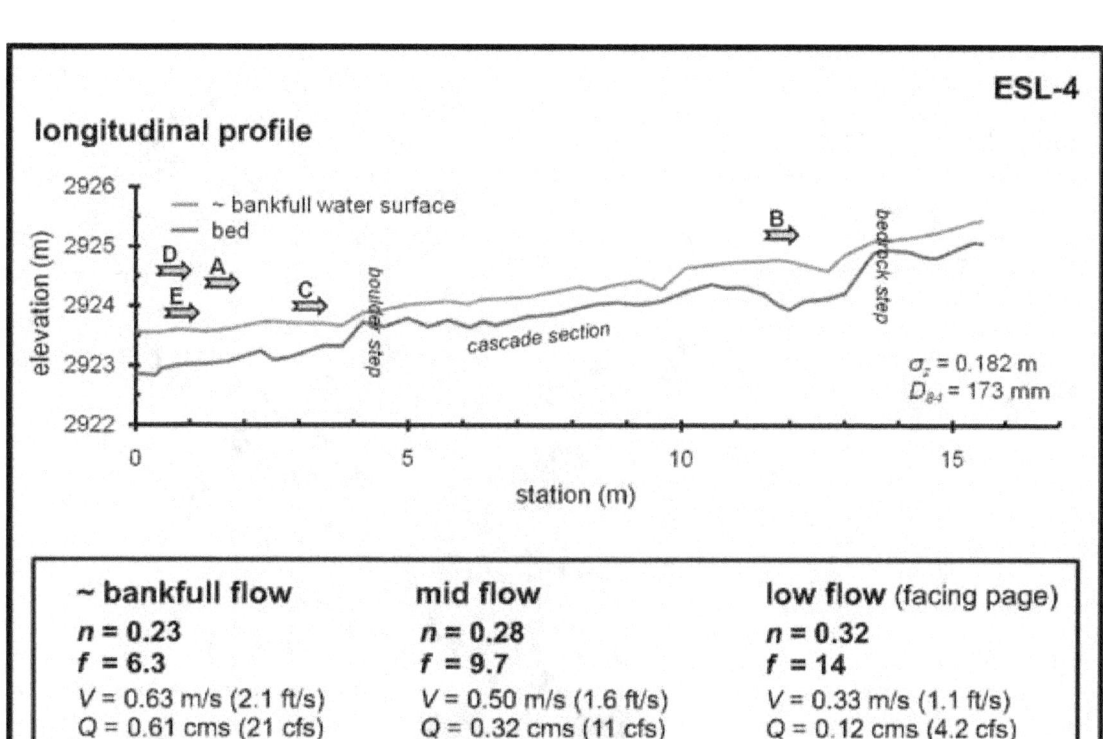

longitudinal profile

ESL-4

~ bankfull water surface
bed

boulder step

cascade section

boulder step

bedrock step

D
A
E
C
B

$\sigma_z = 0.182$ m
$D_{84} = 173$ mm

~ bankfull flow	mid flow	low flow (facing page)
$n = 0.23$	$n = 0.28$	$n = 0.32$
$f = 6.3$	$f = 9.7$	$f = 14$
$V = 0.63$ m/s (2.1 ft/s)	$V = 0.50$ m/s (1.6 ft/s)	$V = 0.33$ m/s (1.1 ft/s)
$Q = 0.61$ cms (21 cfs)	$Q = 0.32$ cms (11 cfs)	$Q = 0.12$ cms (4.2 cfs)
$R = 0.26$ m (0.86 ft)	$R = 0.26$ m (0.85 ft)	$R = 0.17$ m (0.56 ft)
$W = 2.9$ m (9.4 ft)	$W = 2.9$ m (9.4 ft)	$W = 2.3$ m (7.6 ft)
$Fr = 0.34$	$Fr = 0.27$	$Fr = 0.23$

~ bankfull flow   6/7/2008

mid flow   7/14/2008

FC-6 (cascade)

Fool Creek, Colorado, USA

S = 0.20 m/m; W = 1.1 m (3.5 ft); L = 19 m (63 ft)

low flow

8/14/2010

7/17/2008

9/25/2009

Fraser Experimental Forest;
Arapaho-Roosevelt National Forest

stream classification (Rosgen): A4a+

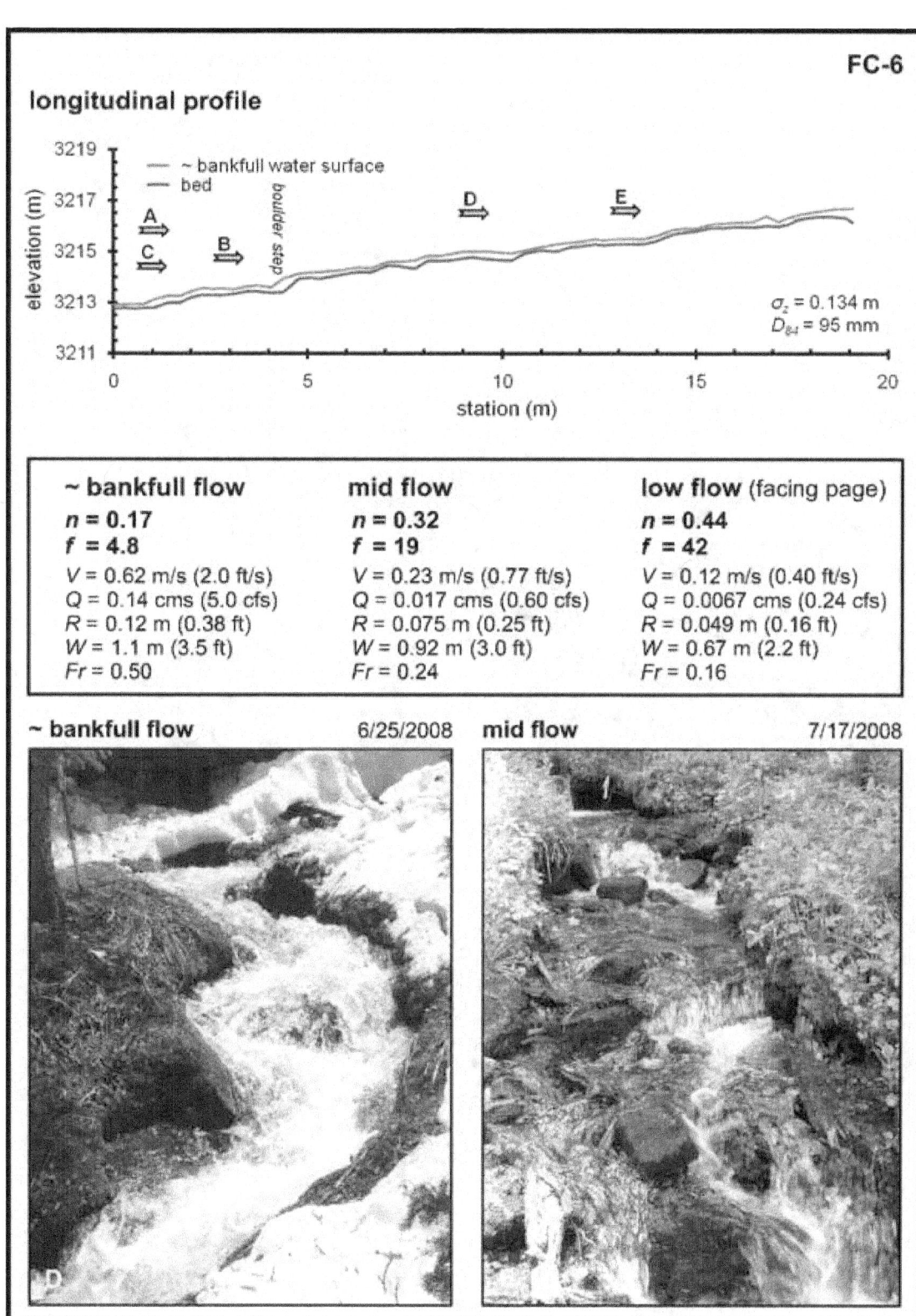

FC-6

longitudinal profile

~ bankfull water surface
bed

A
C
B
boulder step
D
E

$\sigma_z = 0.134$ m
$D_{84} = 95$ mm

elevation (m): 3211, 3213, 3215, 3217, 3219
station (m): 0, 5, 10, 15, 20

~ bankfull flow
$n = 0.17$
$f = 4.8$
$V = 0.62$ m/s (2.0 ft/s)
$Q = 0.14$ cms (5.0 cfs)
$R = 0.12$ m (0.38 ft)
$W = 1.1$ m (3.5 ft)
$Fr = 0.50$

mid flow
$n = 0.32$
$f = 19$
$V = 0.23$ m/s (0.77 ft/s)
$Q = 0.017$ cms (0.60 cfs)
$R = 0.075$ m (0.25 ft)
$W = 0.92$ m (3.0 ft)
$Fr = 0.24$

low flow (facing page)
$n = 0.44$
$f = 42$
$V = 0.12$ m/s (0.40 ft/s)
$Q = 0.0067$ cms (0.24 cfs)
$R = 0.049$ m (0.16 ft)
$W = 0.67$ m (2.2 ft)
$Fr = 0.16$

~ bankfull flow   6/25/2008   **mid flow**   7/17/2008

ESL-5 (step-pool)

East Saint Louis Creek, Colorado, USA
S = 0.16 m/m; W = 4.0 m (13.3 ft); L = 13 m (41 ft)

low flow

9/26/2009

Fraser Experimental Forest;
Arapaho-Roosevelt National Forest
stream classification (Rosgen): B3a

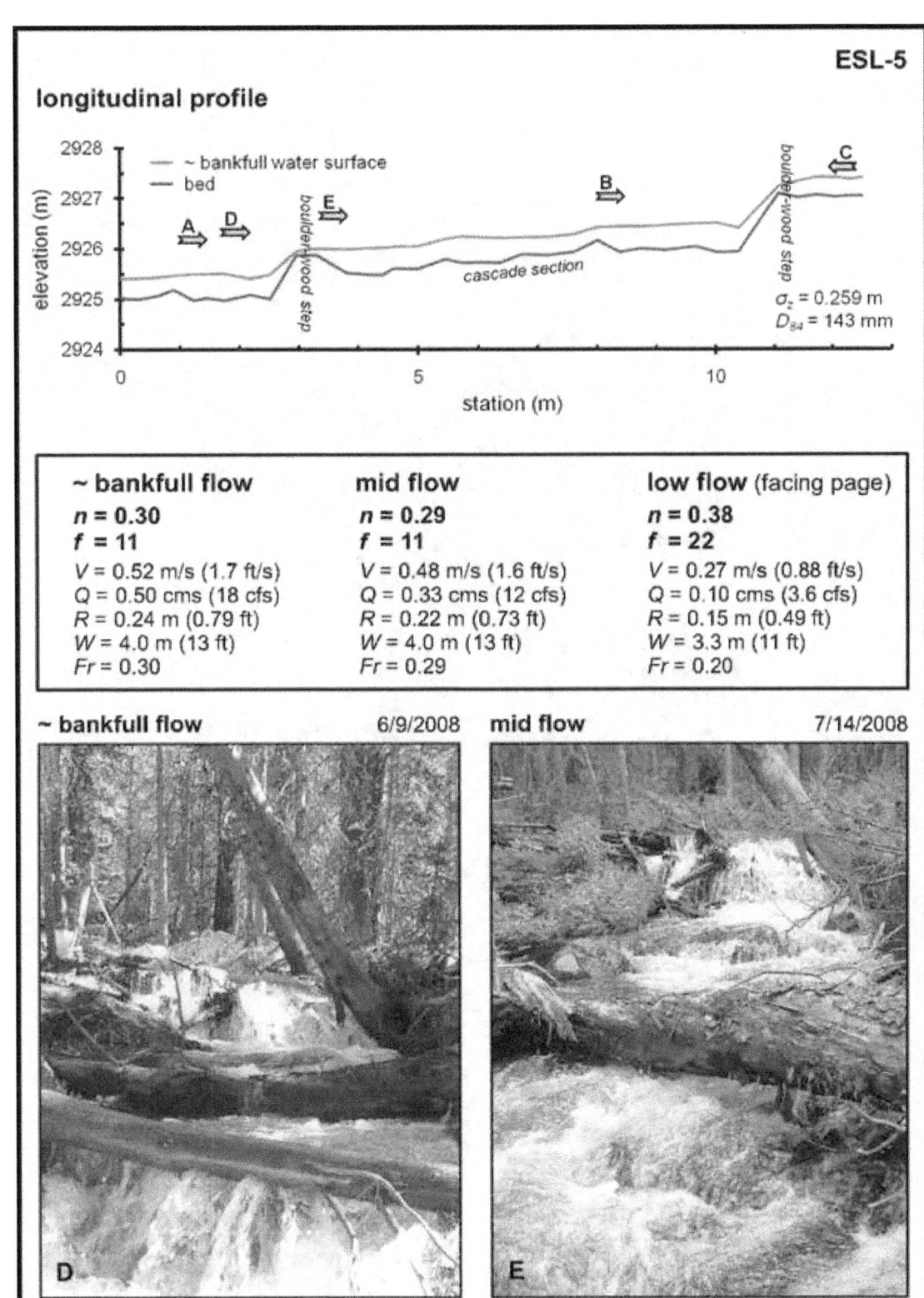

ESL-5

longitudinal profile

σ_z = 0.259 m
D_84 = 143 mm

$\sigma_z = 0.259$ m
$D_{84} = 143$ mm

~ **bankfull flow**	**mid flow**	**low flow** (facing page)
$n = 0.30$	$n = 0.29$	$n = 0.38$
$f = 11$	$f = 11$	$f = 22$
$V = 0.52$ m/s (1.7 ft/s)	$V = 0.48$ m/s (1.6 ft/s)	$V = 0.27$ m/s (0.88 ft/s)
$Q = 0.50$ cms (18 cfs)	$Q = 0.33$ cms (12 cfs)	$Q = 0.10$ cms (3.6 cfs)
$R = 0.24$ m (0.79 ft)	$R = 0.22$ m (0.73 ft)	$R = 0.15$ m (0.49 ft)
$W = 4.0$ m (13 ft)	$W = 4.0$ m (13 ft)	$W = 3.3$ m (11 ft)
$Fr = 0.30$	$Fr = 0.29$	$Fr = 0.20$

~ bankfull flow   6/9/2008   **mid flow**   7/14/2008

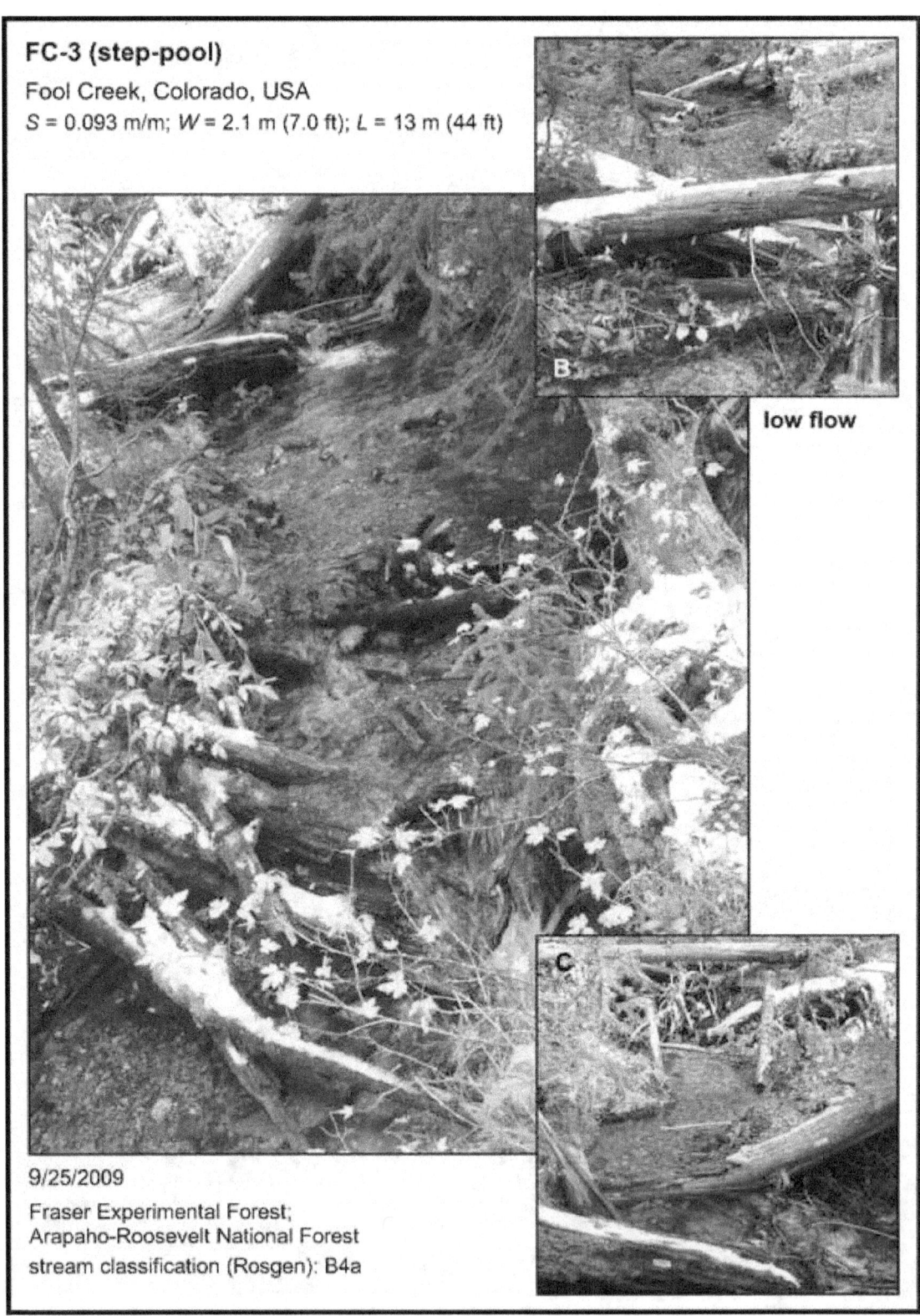

FC-3 (step-pool)

Fool Creek, Colorado, USA

S = 0.093 m/m; W = 2.1 m (7.0 ft); L = 13 m (44 ft)

low flow

9/25/2009

Fraser Experimental Forest;
Arapaho-Roosevelt National Forest

stream classification (Rosgen): B4a

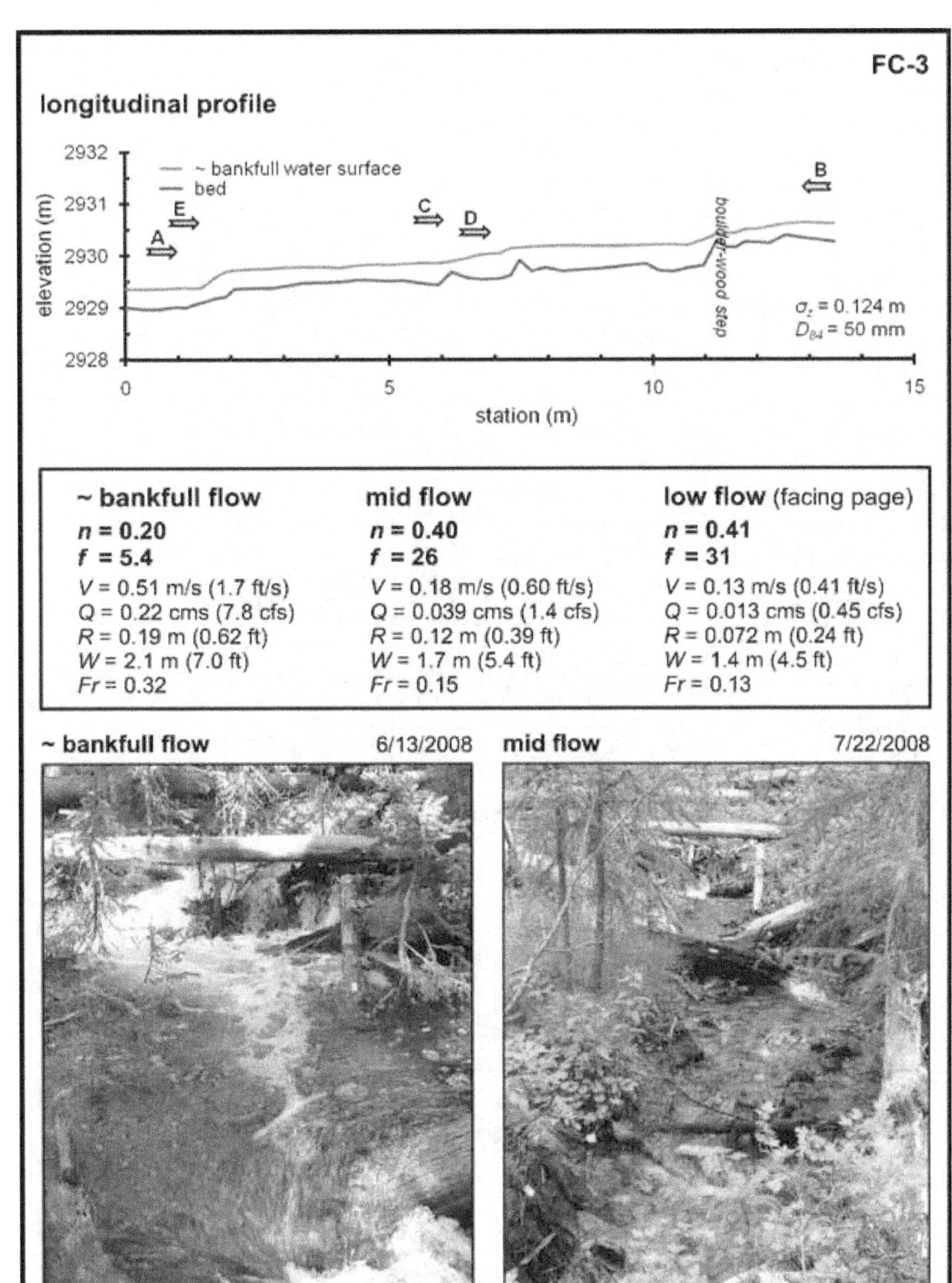

FC-3

longitudinal profile

- ~ bankfull water surface
- bed

σ_z = 0.124 m
D_{84} = 50 mm

~ bankfull flow	**mid flow**	**low flow** (facing page)
n = 0.20	n = 0.40	n = 0.41
f = 5.4	f = 26	f = 31
V = 0.51 m/s (1.7 ft/s)	V = 0.18 m/s (0.60 ft/s)	V = 0.13 m/s (0.41 ft/s)
Q = 0.22 cms (7.8 cfs)	Q = 0.039 cms (1.4 cfs)	Q = 0.013 cms (0.45 cfs)
R = 0.19 m (0.62 ft)	R = 0.12 m (0.39 ft)	R = 0.072 m (0.24 ft)
W = 2.1 m (7.0 ft)	W = 1.7 m (5.4 ft)	W = 1.4 m (4.5 ft)
Fr = 0.32	Fr = 0.15	Fr = 0.13

~ bankfull flow   6/13/2008   **mid flow**   7/22/2008

FC-4 (step-pool)

Fool Creek, Colorado, USA

S = 0.13 m/m; W = 1.6 m (5.2 ft); L = 19 m (62 ft)

low flow

9/26/2009

Fraser Experimental Forest;
Arapaho-Roosevelt National Forest

stream classification (Rosgen): B3a

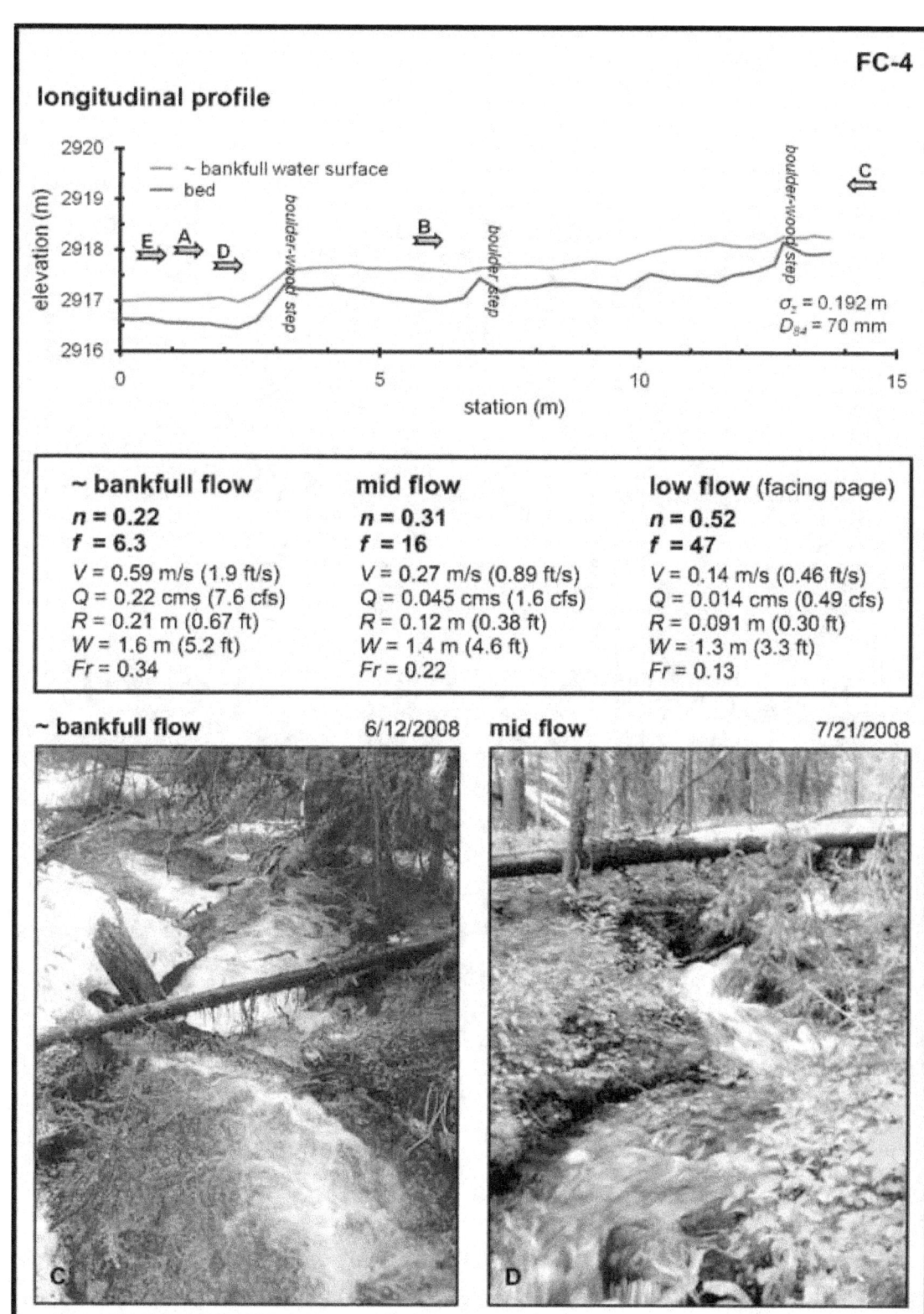

FC-4

longitudinal profile

elevation (m) vs station (m)

- ~ bankfull water surface
- bed

boulder-wood step, boulder step, boulder-wood step

$\sigma_z = 0.192$ m
$D_{84} = 70$ mm

~ bankfull flow
$n = 0.22$
$f = 6.3$
$V = 0.59$ m/s (1.9 ft/s)
$Q = 0.22$ cms (7.6 cfs)
$R = 0.21$ m (0.67 ft)
$W = 1.6$ m (5.2 ft)
$Fr = 0.34$

mid flow
$n = 0.31$
$f = 16$
$V = 0.27$ m/s (0.89 ft/s)
$Q = 0.045$ cms (1.6 cfs)
$R = 0.12$ m (0.38 ft)
$W = 1.4$ m (4.6 ft)
$Fr = 0.22$

low flow (facing page)
$n = 0.52$
$f = 47$
$V = 0.14$ m/s (0.46 ft/s)
$Q = 0.014$ cms (0.49 cfs)
$R = 0.091$ m (0.30 ft)
$W = 1.3$ m (3.3 ft)
$Fr = 0.13$

~ bankfull flow   6/12/2008   **mid flow**   7/21/2008

RC-5 (cascade)

Rio Cordon, Italy

S = 0.21 m/m; W = 5.8 m (19 ft); L = 20 m (64 ft)

low flow

7/29/2004

Dolomite range;
Eastern Italian Alps

stream classification (Rosgen): A2a+

longitudinal profile

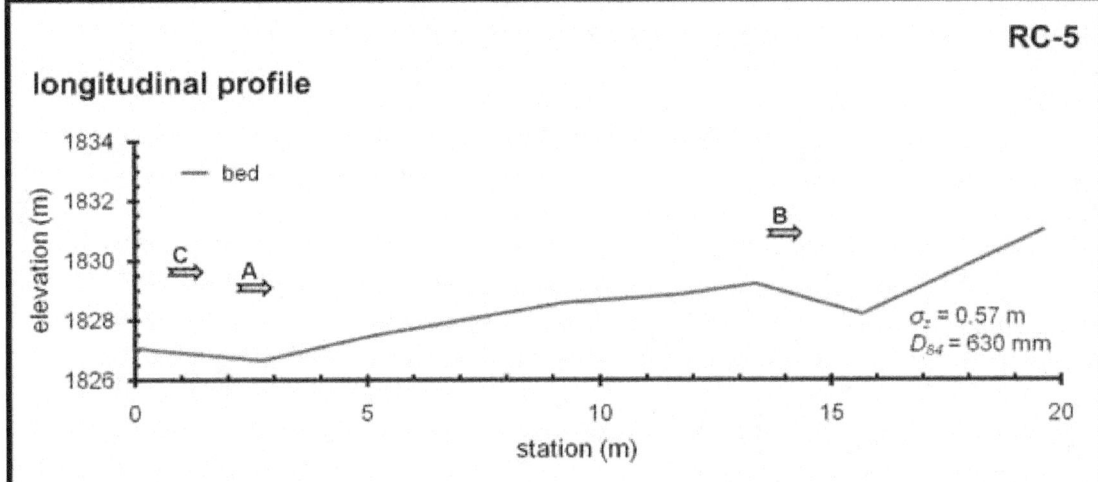

$\sigma_z = 0.57$ m
$D_{84} = 630$ mm

high flow	**low flow** (facing page)
$n = 0.35$	$n = 0.41$
$f = 16$	$f = 28$
$V = 0.50$ m/s (1.6 ft/s)	$V = 0.25$ m/s (0.82 ft/s)
$Q = 1.0$ cms (36 cfs)	$Q = 0.17$ cms (6.0 cfs)
$R = 0.24$ m (0.79 ft)	$R = 0.11$ m (0.36 ft)
$W = 5.8$ m (19 ft)	$W = 2.3$ m (7.5 ft)
$Fr = 0.27$	$Fr = 0.15$

high flow   11/1/2004

mid flow   6/24/2004

Photographic Guidance

Single Discharges

Twenty-eight figures are provided illustrating stream reach characteristics, with Manning's n and Darcy-Weisbach f given for a single discharge (Figures Porter 11 – Bear Creek). This discharge was typically low flow. Single photographs are provided, illustrating conditions when flow resistance was measured. Profile plots are also included, to depict the bed morphology. The figures are ordered from the lowest to the highest resistance.

Figure 5: A transitional plane-bed / step-pool morphology channel without instream wood enhancement of bedforms (Porter River 8).

USDA Forest Service RMRS-GTR-323. 2014.

Porter-11 (plane-bed)

Porter River, South Island, New Zealand
S = 0.013 m/m; W = 5.1 m (17 ft); L = 57 m (186 ft), stream classification (Rosgen): C3

n = 0.057	V = 0.68 m/s (2.2 ft/s)
f = 0.44	R = 0.2 m (0.66 ft)

1/16/2003

longitudinal profile

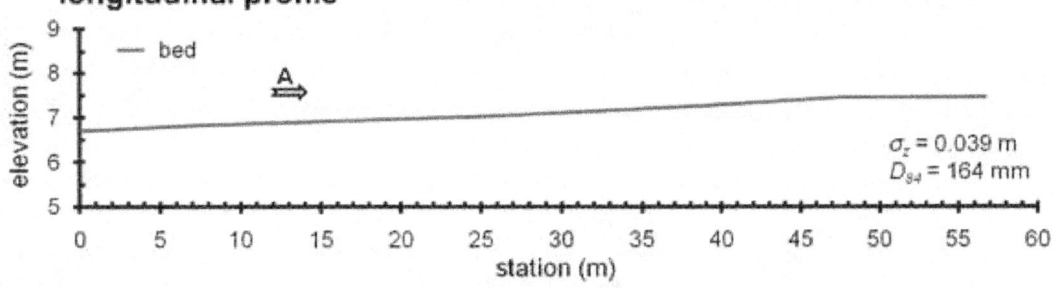

σ_z = 0.039 m
D_{84} = 164 mm

elevation (m)

station (m)

bed

A

BE-A (transitional: plane-bed / step-pool)

Buena Esperanza, Tierra del Fuego, Argentina
S = 0.022 m/m; W = 4.4 m (14 ft); L = 22 m (71 ft), stream classification (Rosgen): B3

n = **0.059** V = 0.77 m/s (2.5 ft/s)
f = **0.50** R = 0.17 m (0.56 ft)

2/13/2006

longitudinal profile

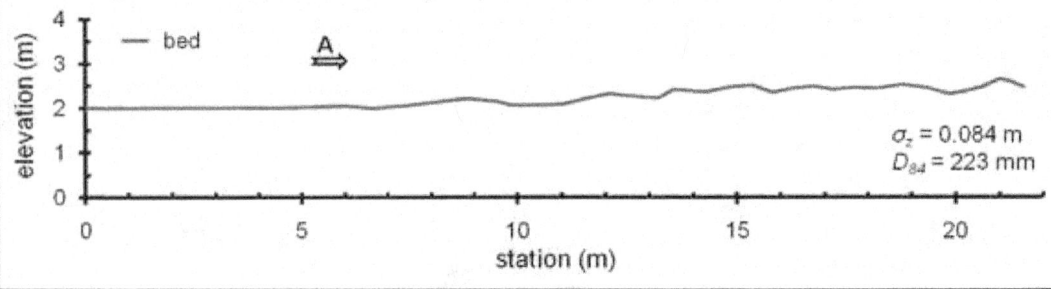

σ_z = 0.084 m
D_{84} = 223 mm

Porter-4 (transitional: plane-bed / step-pool)

Porter River, South Island, New Zealand
S = 0.026 m/m; W = 1.6 m (5.2 ft); L = 35 m (114 ft), stream classification (Rosgen): E3b

n = 0.074	V = 0.74 m/s (2.4 ft/s)
f = 0.74	R = 0.2 m (0.66 ft)

1/16/2003

longitudinal profile

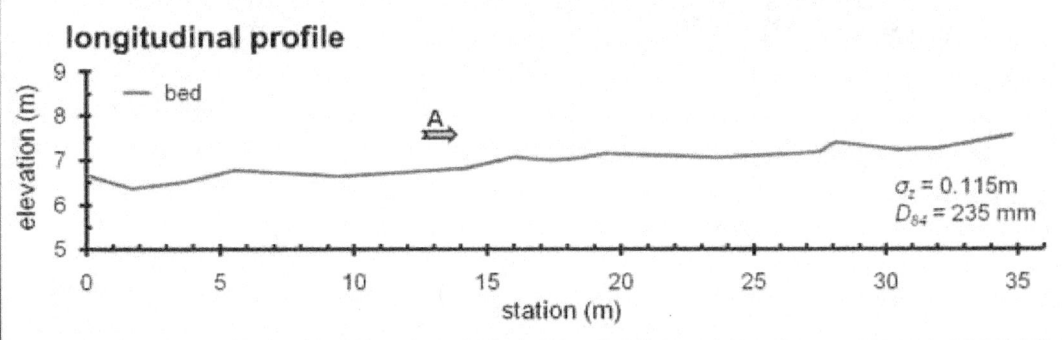

σ_z = 0.115m
D_{84} = 235 mm

BE-C (transitional: plane-bed / riffle-glide)

Buena Esperanza, Tierra del Fuego, Argentina
S = 0.023 m/m; W = 4.2 m (14 ft); L = 17 m (57 ft), stream classification (Rosgen): B3

n = 0.081	V = 0.56 m/s (1.8 ft/s)
f = 0.94	R = 0.16 m (0.52 ft)

2/13/2006

longitudinal profile

σ_z = 0.232 m
D_{84} = 133 mm

Porter-6 (transitional: plane-bed / step-pool)

Porter River, South Island, New Zealand
S = 0.047 m/m; W = 3.3 m (11 ft); L = 56 m (183 ft), stream classification (Rosgen): B3a

n = **0.091**	V = 0.81 m/s (2.7 ft/s)
f = **1.1**	R = 0.2 m (0.66 ft)

1/16/2003

longitudinal profile

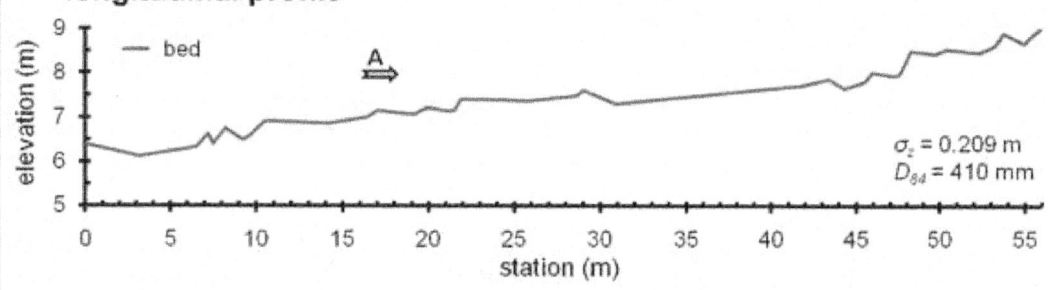

σ_z = 0.209 m
D_{84} = 410 mm

Porter-9 (transitional: plane-bed / step-pool)

Porter River, South Island, New Zealand
S = 0.036 m/m; W = 5.4 m (18 ft); L = 54 m (176 ft), stream classification (Rosgen): B4

n = 0.11 V = 0.57 m/s (1.9 ft/s)
f = 1.7 R = 0.2 m (0.66 ft)

1/16/2003

longitudinal profile

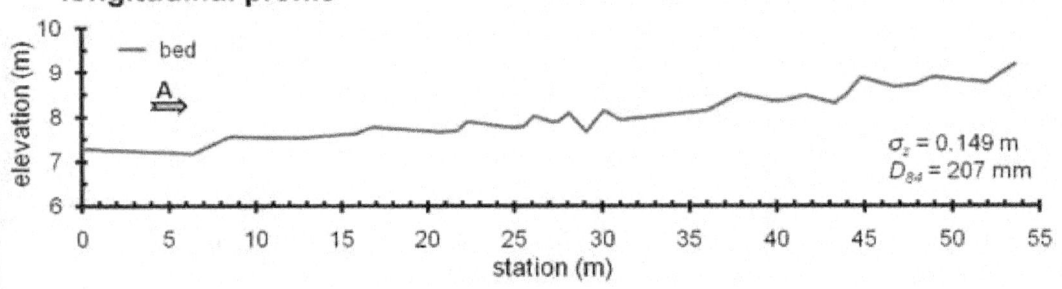

σ_z = 0.149 m
D_{84} = 207 mm

Porter-8 (transitional: plane-bed / step-pool)

Porter River, South Island, New Zealand
S = 0.045 m/m; W = 5.1 m (17 ft); L = 50 m (164 ft), stream classification (Rosgen): B3a

n = 0.13	V = 0.55 m/s (1.8 ft/s)
f = 2.3	R = 0.2 m (0.66 ft)

1/16/2003

longitudinal profile

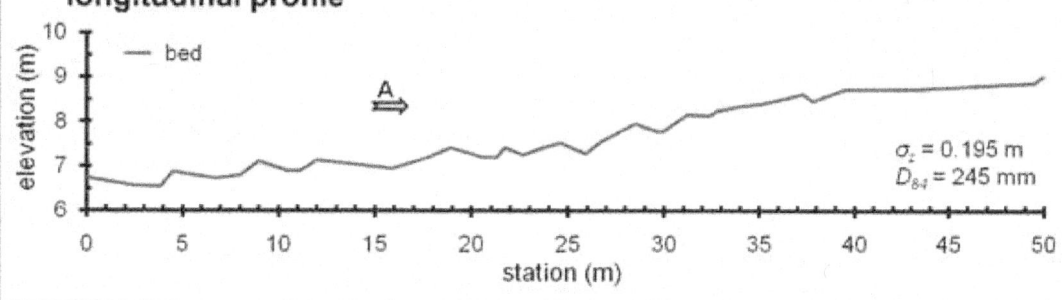

σ_z = 0.195 m
D_{84} = 245 mm

TA-15 (transitional: pool-riffle / step-pool)

Tres Arroyos, Malalcahuello National Preserve, Chile
S = 0.028 m/m; W = 3.6 m (12 ft); L = 41 m (135 ft), stream classification (Rosgen): B3

n = **0.13** V = 0.31 m/s (1.0 ft/s)
f = **2.7** R = 0.12 m (0.39 ft)

4/7/2005

longitudinal profile

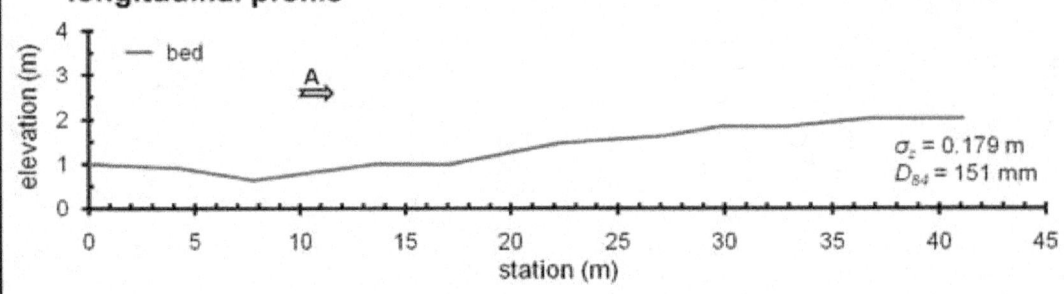

σ_z = 0.179 m
D_{84} = 151 mm

Kowai-8 (transitional: plane-bed / step-pool)

Kowai River, South Island, New Zealand
S = 0.064 m/m; W = 2.6 m (8.5 ft); L = 33 m (108 ft), stream classification (Rosgen): B4a

n = 0.14	V = 0.4 m/s (1.3 ft/s)
f = 3.1	R = 0.1 m (0.33 ft)

1/28/2003

longitudinal profile

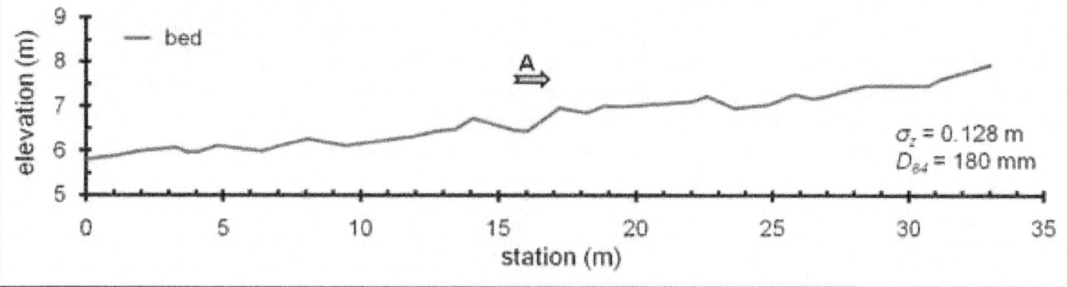

σ_z = 0.128 m
D_{84} = 180 mm

elevation (m)

— bed

A

station (m)

Camp-5 (cascade)

Camp Creek, South Island, New Zealand
S = 0.10 m/m; W = 6.7 m (22 ft); L = 47 m (154 ft), stream classification (Rosgen): A2

n = 0.19	V = 0.35 m/s (1.1 ft/s)
f = 6.4	R = 0.1 m (0.33 ft)

3/14/2003

longitudinal profile

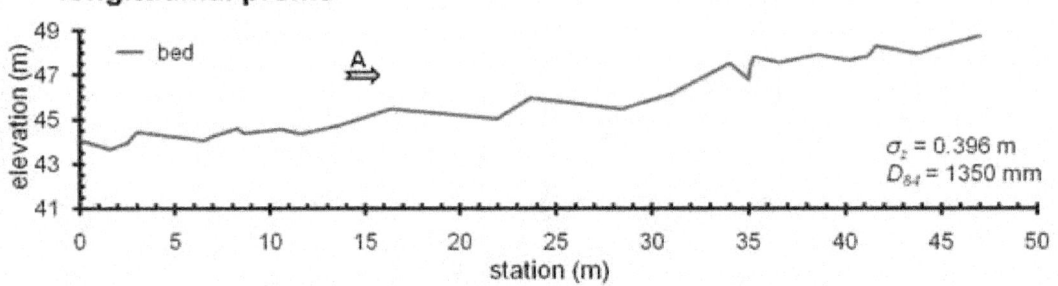

σ_z = 0.396 m
D_{84} = 1350 mm

Camp-2 (step-pool)

Camp Creek, South Island, New Zealand
S = 0.16 m/m; W = 6.0 m (20 ft); L = 46 m (151 ft), stream classification (Rosgen): A2a+

n = 0.22	V = 0.38 m/s (1.2 ft/s)
f = 8.6	R = 0.1 m (0.33 ft)

3/14/2003

longitudinal profile

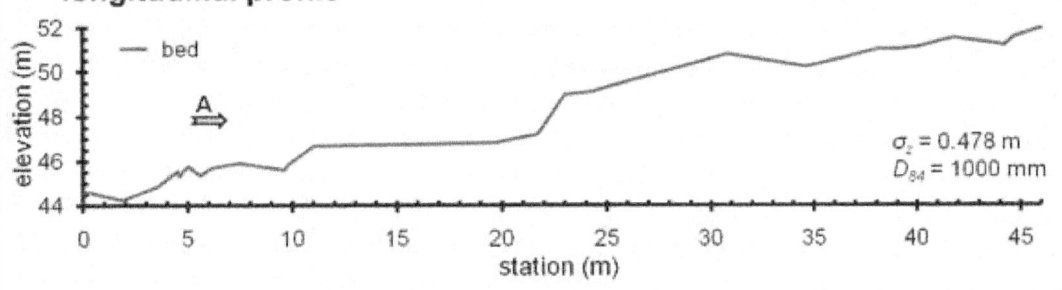

σ_z = 0.478 m
D_{84} = 1000 mm

Lower Kellogg Creek (step-pool)

Puyallup River Watershed, Washington State, USA
S = 0.061 m/m; W = 2.1 m (7.0 ft); L = 48 m (158 ft), stream classification (Rosgen): B3a

n = **0.25**	V = 0.18 m/s (0.59 ft/s)
f = **11**	R = 0.076 m (0.25 ft)

7/7/1999

longitudinal profile

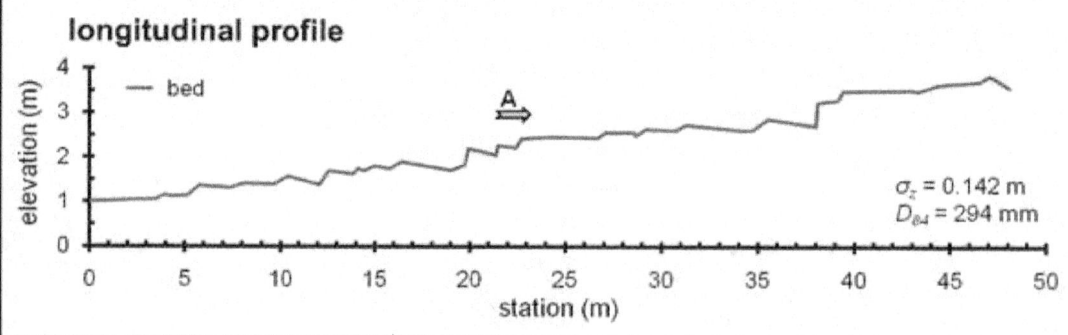

σ_z = 0.142 m
D_{84} = 294 mm

BE-E (cascade)

Buena Esperanza, Tierra del Fuego, Argentina
S = 0.076 m/m; W = 4.6 m (15 ft); L = 23 m (77 ft), stream classification (Rosgen): B3a

n = 0.25	V = 0.37 m/s (1.2 ft/s)
f = 8.3	R = 0.19 m (0.62 ft)

3/5/2006

longitudinal profile

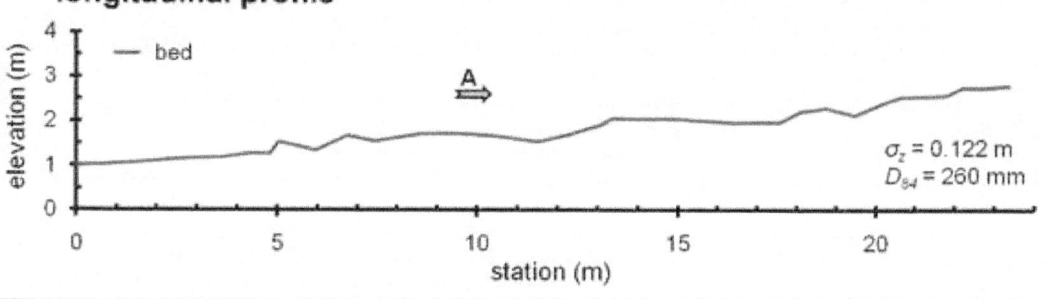

σ_z = 0.122 m
D_{84} = 260 mm

TA-14 (transitional: step-pool / cascade)

Tres Arroyos, Malalcahuello National Preserve, Chile
S = 0.072 m/m; W = 3.0 m (10 ft); L = 99 m (324 ft), stream classification (Rosgen): A3

n = 0.26	V = 0.26 m/s (0.85 ft/s)
f = 11	R = 0.13 m (0.43 ft)

4/7/2005

longitudinal profile

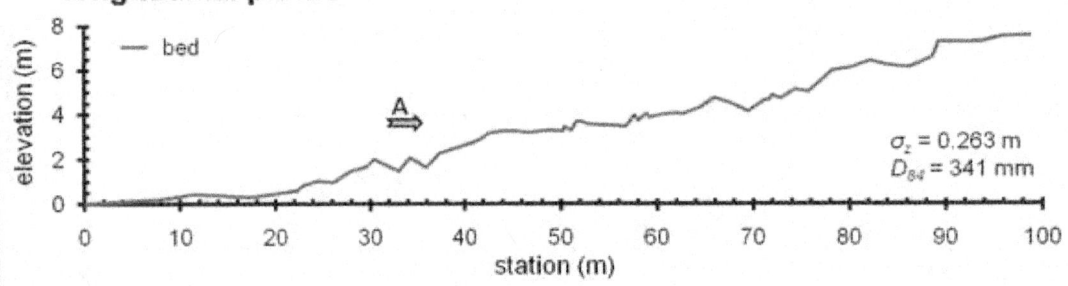

σ_z = 0.263 m
D_{84} = 341 mm

BE-G (step-pool)

Buena Esperanza, Tierra del Fuego, Argentina
S = 0.10 m/m; W = 2.8 m (9.1 ft); L = 17 m (55 ft), stream classification (Rosgen): A3a+

n = 0.27	V = 0.39 m/s (1.3 ft/s)
f = 10	R = 0.19 m (0.62 ft)

3/5/2006

longitudinal profile

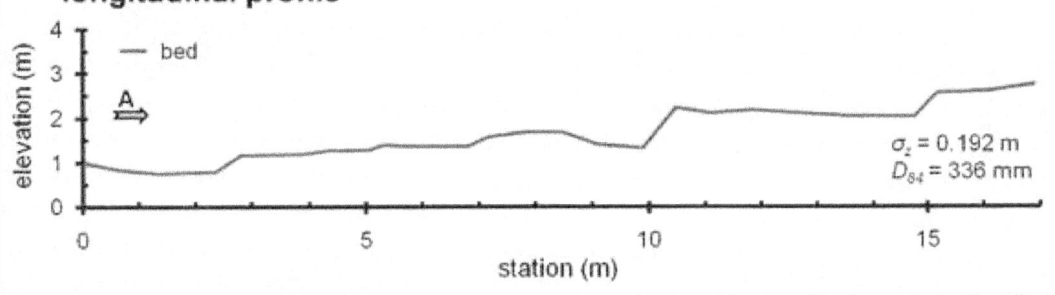

σ_z = 0.192 m
D_{84} = 336 mm

S.F. Mashel, lower (step-pool)

Nisqually River Watershed, Washington State, USA
S = 0.051 m/m; W = 2.6 m (8.7 ft); L = 58 m (192 ft), stream classification (Rosgen): B3a

n = 0.31	V = 0.17 m/s (0.55 ft/s)
f = 16	R = 0.11 m (0.36 ft)

7/27/1999

longitudinal profile

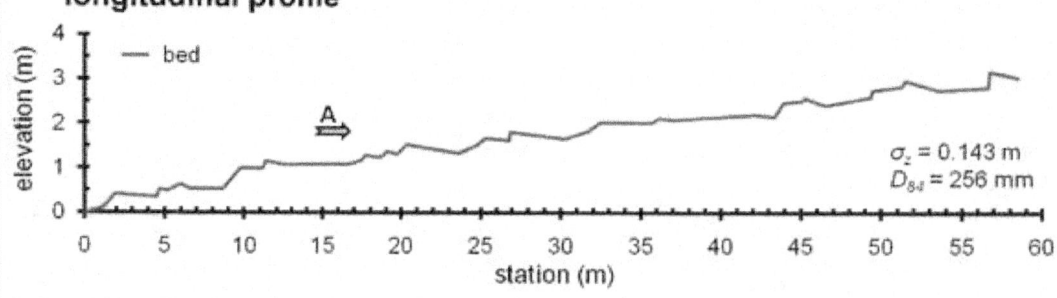

σ_z = 0.143 m
D_{84} = 256 mm

USDA Forest Service RMRS-GTR-323. 2014.

Camp-7 (step-pool)

Camp Creek, South Island, New Zealand
S = 0.19 m/m; W = 2.7 m (8.9 ft); L = 30 m (98 ft), stream classification (Rosgen): A2a+

n = 0.34	V = 0.27 m/s (0.89 ft/s)
f = 20	R = 0.1 m (0.33 ft)

2/10/2003

longitudinal profile

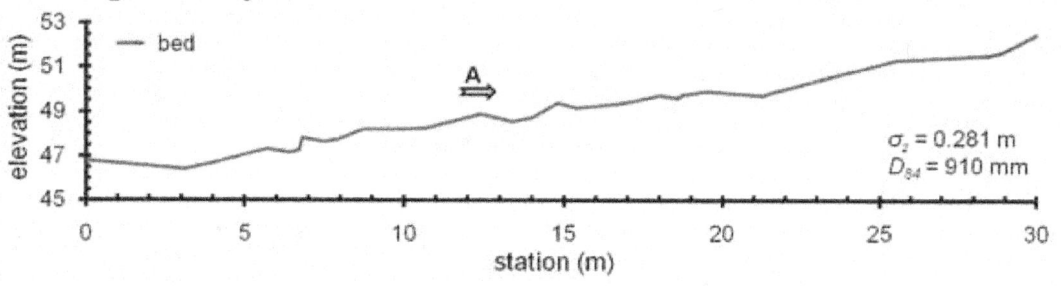

σ_z = 0.281 m
D_{84} = 910 mm

Lost Creek (step-pool)

Puyallup River Watershed, Washington State, USA
S = 0.12 m/m; W = 2.3 m (7.5 ft); L = 54 m (176 ft), stream classification (Rosgen): A3a+

n = **0.35**	V = 0.25 m/s (0.82 ft/s)
f = **19**	R = 0.13 m (0.43 ft)

7/10/1997

longitudinal profile

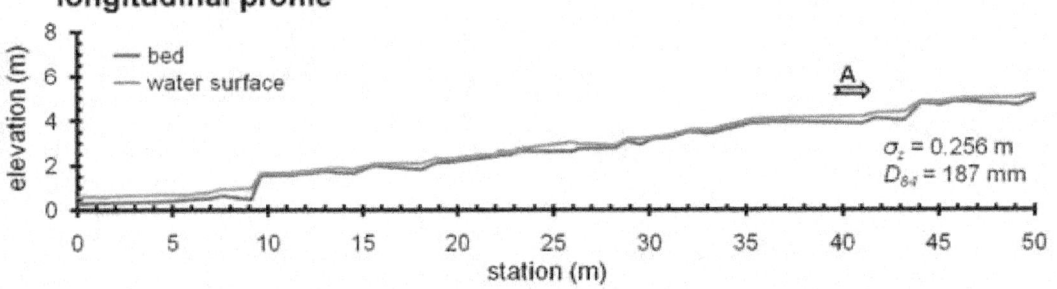

bed
water surface

A

σ_z = 0.256 m
D_{84} = 187 mm

Kowai-1 (step-pool)

Kowai River, South Island, New Zealand
S = 0.18 m/m; W = 3.2 m (10 ft); L = 46 m (151 ft), stream classification (Rosgen): A3a+

n = 0.36	V = 0.25 m/s (0.82 ft/s)
f = 23	R = 0.1 m (0.33 ft)

2/11/2003

longitudinal profile

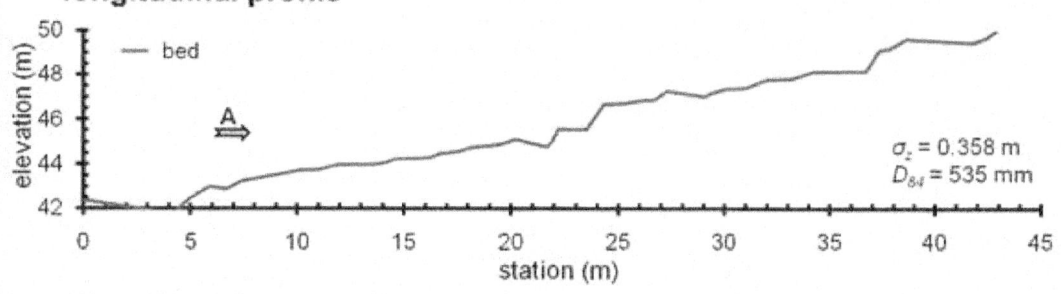

σ_z = 0.358 m
D_{84} = 535 mm

Spine Creek (transitional: step-pool / cascade)

Puyallup River Watershed, Washington State, USA
S = 0.12 m/m; W = 1.5 m (4.9 ft); L = 53 m (174 ft), stream classification (Rosgen): B3a

n = 0.38	V = 0.16 m/s (0.52 ft/s)
f = 27	R = 0.077 m (0.25 ft)

11/25/1997

longitudinal profile

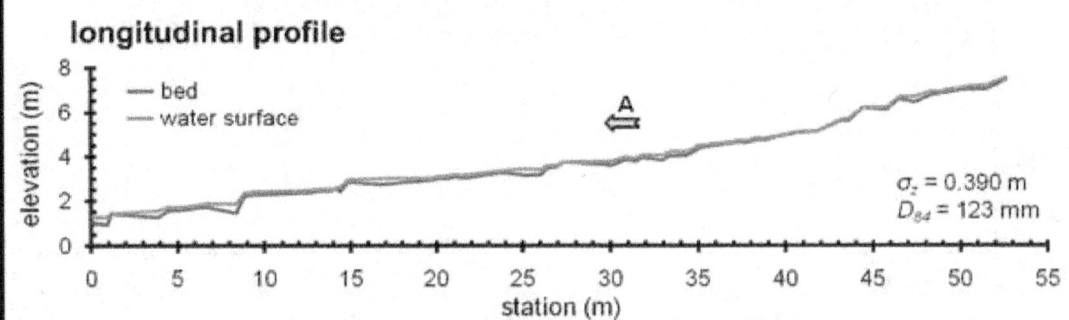

σ_z = 0.390 m
D_{84} = 123 mm

S.F. Mashel, upper (step-pool)

Nisqually River Watershed, Washington State, USA
S = 0.12 m/m; W = 1.3 m (4.1 ft); L = 52 m (169 ft), stream classification (Rosgen): B3a

n = **0.45**	V = 0.12 m/s (0.39 ft/s)
f = **40**	R = 0.060 m (0.20 ft)

7/27/1999

longitudinal profile

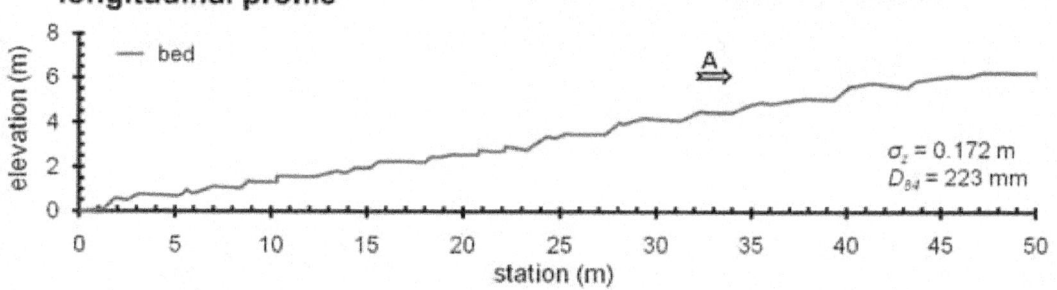

σ_z = 0.172 m
D_{84} = 223 mm

N. F. Busywild Creek (step-pool)

Nisqually River Watershed, Washington State, USA
S = 0.083 m/m; W = 1.4 m (4.5 ft); L = 56 m (182 ft), stream classification (Rosgen): A3

n = 0.48	V = 0.12 m/s (0.38 ft/s)
f = 41	R = 0.085 m (0.28 ft)

7/8/1999

longitudinal profile

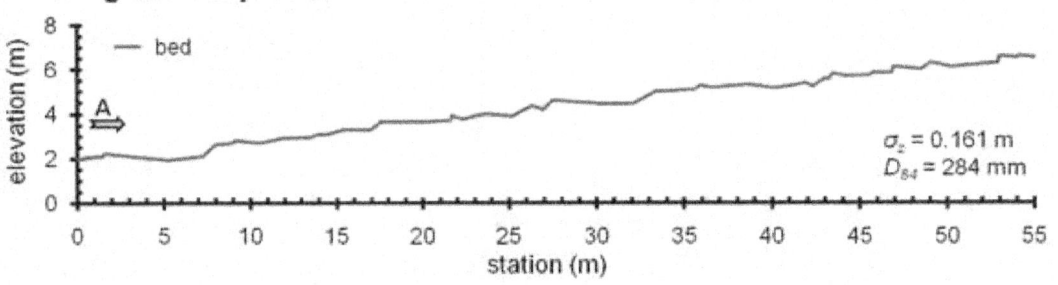

σ_z = 0.161 m
D_{84} = 284 mm

USDA Forest Service RMRS-GTR-323. 2014.

Caterpillar Creek (step-pool)

Cowlitz River Watershed, Washington State, USA
S = 0.14 m/m; W = 0.94 m (3.1 ft); L = 55 m (182 ft), stream classification (Rosgen): B3a

n = 0.52	V = 0.094 m/s (0.31 ft/s)
f = 59	R = 0.047 m (0.15 ft)

7/24/1999

longitudinal profile

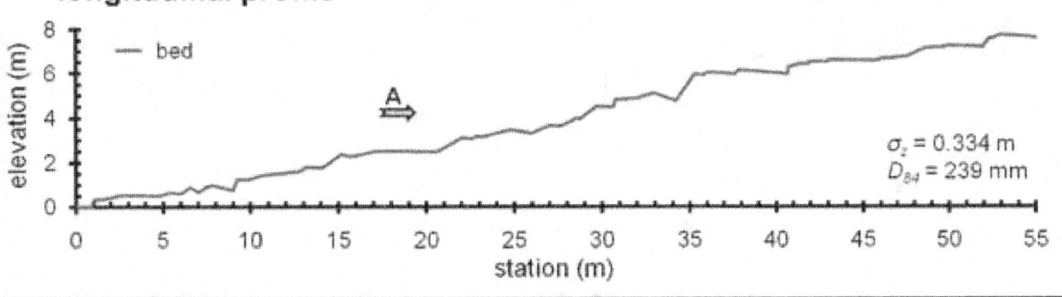

σ_z = 0.334 m
D_{84} = 239 mm

McLaine Creek (step-pool)

Yakima River Watershed, Washington State, USA
S = 0.18 m/m; W = 2.0 m (6.6 ft); L = 48 m (156 ft), stream classification (Rosgen): A3a+

n = 0.55	V = 0.21 m/s (0.69 ft/s)
f = 45	R = 0.14 m (0.46 ft)

6/25/1997

longitudinal profile

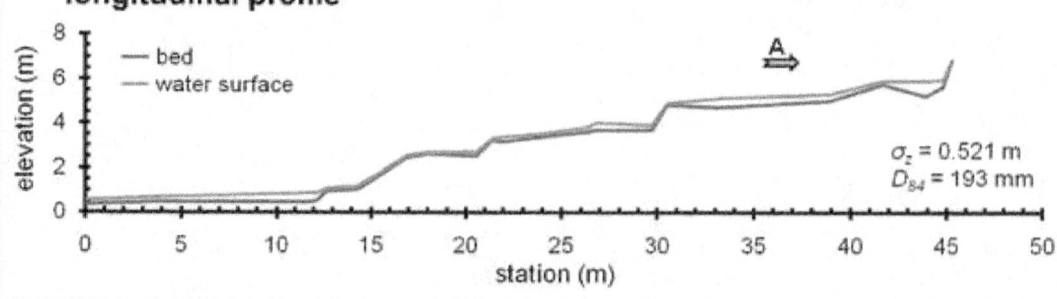

σ_z = 0.521 m
D_{84} = 193 mm

Tacoma Creek, upper (step-pool)

Cowlitz River Watershed, Washington State, USA
S = 0.099 m/m; W = 2.3 m (7.6 ft); L = 51 m (168 ft), stream classification (Rosgen): B3a

n = **0.65** V = 0.11 m/s (0.36 ft/s)
f = **71** R = 0.11 m (0.35 ft)

7/22/1999

longitudinal profile

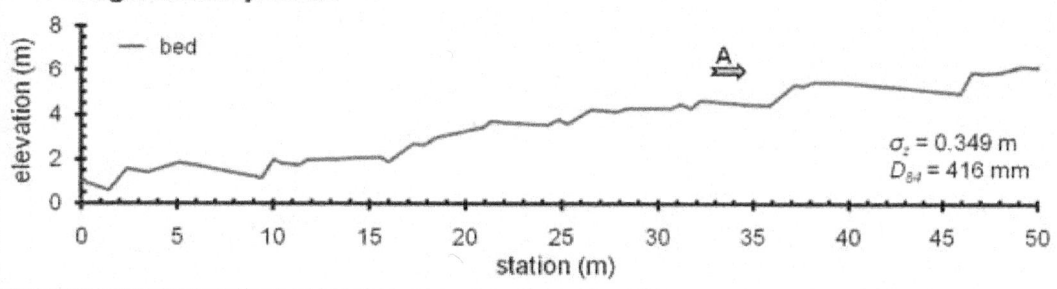

σ_z = 0.349 m
D_{84} = 416 mm

Hard Creek (transitional: step-pool / cascade)

Deschutes River Watershed, Washington State, USA
S = 0.093 m/m; W = 3.2 m (10 ft); L = 61 m (200 ft), stream classification (Rosgen): A3

n = 0.74	V = 0.13 m/s (0.43 ft/s)
f = 76	R = 0.18 m (0.59 ft)

7/15/1997

longitudinal profile

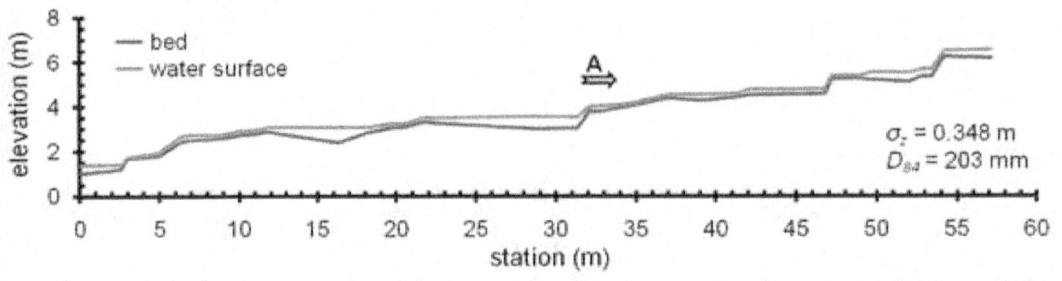

σ_z = 0.348 m
D_{84} = 203 mm

USDA Forest Service RMRS-GTR-323. 2014.

TA-10 (step-pool)

Tres Arroyos, Malalcahuello National Preserve, Chile
S = 0.15 m/m; W = 5.3 m (17 ft); L = 32 m (104 ft), stream classification (Rosgen): A3a+

n = 0.87	V = 0.11 m/s (0.36 ft/s)
f = 118	R = 0.13 m (0.43 ft)

4/2/2005

longitudinal profile

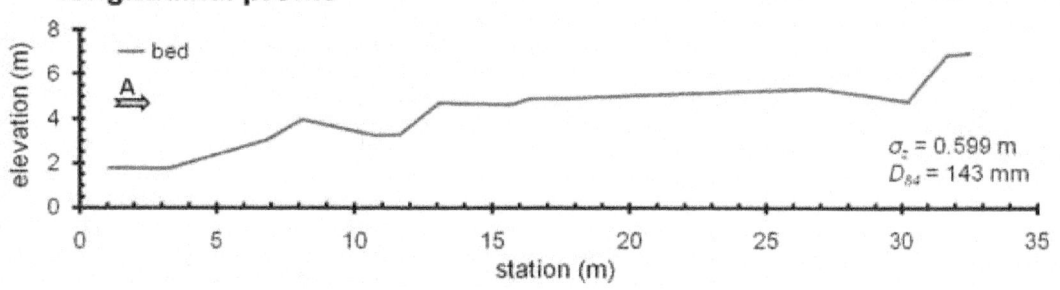

σ_z = 0.599 m
D_{84} = 143 mm

Bear Creek (step-pool)

Yakima River Watershed, Washington State, USA
S = 0.11 m/m; W = 1.7 m (5.6 ft); L = 74 m (244 ft), stream classification (Rosgen): A3a+

n = 0.96	V = 0.079 m/s (0.26 ft/s)
f = 152	R = 0.11 m (0.36 ft)

6/23/1997

longitudinal profile

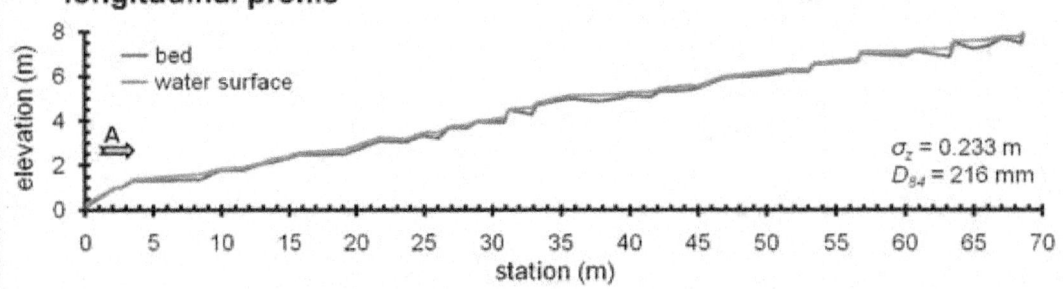

σ_z = 0.233 m
D_{84} = 216 mm

APPENDIX A: Measured Values, Multiple Discharge Reaches

Reach	Flow Type	Reference	Date of Measurement	Slope (m/m)	n	f	V (m/s)	Q (m³/s)	W (m)	L (m)
ESL-6	~bankfull flow	Yochum et al. 2012	6/9/2008	0.024	0.048	0.28	1.32	0.52	3.0	6.4
ESL-6	mid flow	Yochum et al. 2012	7/14/2008	0.015	0.078	0.76	0.61	0.32	2.9	6.4
ESL-6	low flow	Yochum et al. 2012	8/8/2007	0.019	0.099	1.4	0.39	0.10	2.7	6.2
FC-1	~bankfull flow	Yochum et al. 2012	6/11/2008	0.063	0.095	1.3	0.79	0.23	2.0	23.1
FC-1	mid flow	Yochum et al. 2012	7/5/2007	0.061	0.134	3.0	0.40	0.05	1.6	23.7
FC-1	low flow	Yochum et al. 2012	8/12/2007	0.057	0.196	7.6	0.19	0.01	1.3	25.1
RC-1a	high flow	Comiti et al. 2007	11/1/2004	0.079	0.130	1.8	1.14	1.86	4.8	24.6
RC-1a	mid flow	Comiti et al. 2007	10/29/2004	0.079	0.183	4.7	0.48	0.47	4.2	24.6
RC-1a	low flow	Comiti et al. 2007	10/27/2004	0.079	0.178	5.0	0.39	0.21	4.1	24.6
RC-2a	high flow	Comiti et al. 2007	11/1/2004	0.096	0.14	2.2	1.10	1.37	5.7	29.3
RC-2a	mid flow	Comiti et al. 2007	10/29/2004	0.096	0.16	3.9	0.54	0.45	4.2	29.3
RC-2a	low flow	Comiti et al. 2007	7/29/2004	0.096	0.19	6.3	0.31	0.17	1.9	29.3
FC-2	~bankfull flow	Yochum et al. 2012	6/11/2008	0.071	0.13	2.2	0.66	0.24	1.6	14.4
FC-2	mid flow	Yochum et al. 2012	7/23/2008	0.072	0.22	8.0	0.28	0.04	1.4	14.2
FC-2	low flow	Yochum et al. 2012	8/12/2007	0.068	0.24	11.4	0.17	0.013	1.1	14.9
ESL-7	~bankfull flow	Yochum et al. 2012	6/8/2008	0.085	0.17	3.5	0.69	0.52	3.0	22.1
ESL-7	mid flow	Yochum et al. 2012	7/15/2008	0.081	0.19	4.8	0.55	0.30	2.9	24.0
ESL-7	low flow	Yochum et al. 2012	8/4/2007	0.082	0.20	6.0	0.40	0.10	2.5	24.3
ESL-3	~bankfull flow	Yochum et al. 2012	6/7/2008	0.129	0.16	3.7	0.71	0.46	3.6	10.2
ESL-3	mid flow	Yochum et al. 2012	7/15/2008	0.119	0.20	5.7	0.54	0.30	3.5	10.7
ESL-3	low flow	Yochum et al. 2012	8/9/2007	0.119	0.25	9.2	0.38	0.089	2.4	11.3
ESL-8	~bankfull flow	Yochum et al. 2012	6/9/2008	0.094	0.18	4.2	0.64	0.46	3.2	30.7
ESL-8	mid flow	Yochum et al. 2012	7/16/2008	0.087	0.20	5.3	0.53	0.29	3.0	32.6
ESL-8	low flow	Yochum et al. 2012	8/5/2007	0.081	0.24	8.2	0.35	0.10	2.6	35.5
RC-1b	high flow	Comiti et al. 2007	11/1/2004	0.184	0.12	1.6	1.61	1.62	5.4	15.9
RC-1b	mid flow	Comiti et al. 2007	5/24/2004	0.184	0.24	7.4	0.64	0.89	3.8	15.9
RC-1b	low flow	Comiti et al. 2007	7/29/2004	0.184	0.30	16.2	0.28	0.17	2.9	15.9
ESL-1	~bankfull flow	Yochum et al. 2012	6/10/2008	0.095	0.19	4.5	0.65	0.56	2.9	29.4
ESL-1	mid flow	Yochum et al. 2012	7/22/2008	0.105	0.27	9.4	0.42	0.24	2.6	27.3
RC-3	high flow	Comiti et al. 2007	5/30/2004	0.136	0.20	4.5	0.86	0.93	3.8	38.2
RC-3	mid flow	Comiti et al. 2007	10/29/2004	0.136	0.25	8.3	0.50	0.47	3.5	38.2
RC-3	low flow	Comiti et al. 2007	10/27/2004	0.136	0.24	8.9	0.37	0.21	3.3	38.2
ESL-9	~bankfull flow	Yochum et al. 2012	6/8/2008	0.115	0.21	5.5	0.64	0.57	2.8	16.3
ESL-9	mid flow	Yochum et al. 2012	7/11/2007	0.103	0.26	8.8	0.43	0.20	2.6	16.2
ESL-9	low flow	Yochum et al. 2012	8/6/2007	0.090	0.28	10.9	0.33	0.11	2.3	18.6
ESL-2	~bankfull flow	Yochum et al. 2012	6/6/2008	0.094	0.20	4.8	0.61	0.53	3.2	13.7
ESL-2	mid flow	Yochum et al. 2012	7/9/2007	0.093	0.23	7.0	0.45	0.22	2.9	13.9
ESL-2	low flow	Yochum et al. 2012	8/9/2007	0.099	0.39	22.1	0.24	0.09	2.6	13.6
ESL-4	~bankfull flow	Yochum et al. 2012	6/7/2008	0.120	0.23	6.3	0.63	0.61	2.9	15.6
ESL-4	mid flow	Yochum et al. 2012	7/14/2008	0.118	0.28	9.7	0.50	0.32	2.9	15.9
ESL-4	low flow	Yochum et al. 2012	8/6/2007	0.119	0.32	14.4	0.33	0.12	2.3	16.5
FC-6	~bankfull flow	Yochum et al. 2012	6/25/2008	0.200	0.17	4.8	0.62	0.14	1.1	19.1
FC-6	mid flow	Yochum et al. 2012	7/17/2008	0.178	0.32	18.9	0.23	0.02	0.9	20.6
FC-6	low flow	Yochum et al. 2012	8/10/2007	0.165	0.44	41.9	0.12	0.01	0.7	22.1
ESL-5	~bankfull flow	Yochum et al. 2012	6/9/2008	0.160	0.30	11.1	0.52	0.50	4.0	12.5
ESL-5	mid flow	Yochum et al. 2012	7/14/2008	0.143	0.29	10.8	0.48	0.33	4.0	13.9
ESL-5	low flow	Yochum et al. 2012	8/8/2007	0.134	0.38	21.8	0.27	0.10	3.3	15.1
FC-3	~bankfull flow	Yochum et al. 2012	6/12/2008	0.092	0.20	5.4	0.51	0.22	2.1	13.5
FC-3	mid flow	Yochum et al. 2012	7/22/2008	0.099	0.40	26.3	0.18	0.04	1.7	12.2
FC-3	low flow	Yochum et al. 2012	8/11/2007	0.087	0.41	31.4	0.12	0.01	1.4	14.9
FC-4	~bankfull flow	Yochum et al. 2012	6/12/2008	0.135	0.22	6.3	0.59	0.22	1.6	18.9
FC-4	mid flow	Yochum et al. 2012	7/21/2008	0.127	0.31	15.8	0.27	0.05	1.4	19.8
FC-4	low flow	Yochum et al. 2012	8/11/2007	0.132	0.52	46.9	0.14	0.01	1.2	19.2
RC-5	high flow	Comiti et al. 2007	5/28/2004	0.208	0.35	15.6	0.50	1.02	5.8	19.6
RC-5	low flow	Comiti et al. 2007	7/30/2004	0.208	0.41	27.7	0.25	0.17	2.3	19.6

Reach	Flow Type	R (m)	h_m (m)	A (m²)	Fr	D_{50} (mm)	D_{84} (mm)	s_z (m)	Stream Type M&B (1997)	Rosgen
ESL-6	~bankfull flow	0.26	0.38	0.89	0.77	22	77	0.037		
ESL-6	mid flow	0.24	0.35	0.79	0.37	22	77	0.029	plane bed	B3
ESL-6	low flow	0.15	0.21	0.44	0.31	22	77	0.036		
FC-1	~bankfull flow	0.16	0.29	0.38	0.58	32	84	0.063		
FC-1	mid flow	0.10	0.18	0.18	0.38	32	84	0.076	plane-bed / step-pool	A4
FC-1	low flow	0.06	0.12	0.09	0.23	32	84	0.076		
RC-1a	high flow	0.38	----	1.63	0.63	140	460	0.25		
RC-1a	mid flow	0.18	----	0.97	0.32	140	460	0.25	plane-bed / step-pool	B3a
RC-1a	low flow	0.12	----	0.54	0.35	140	460	0.25		
RC-2a	high flow	0.36	----	1.24	0.76	200	510	0.25		
RC-2a	mid flow	0.15	----	0.84	0.38	200	510	0.25	step-pool	A3
RC-2a	low flow	0.08	----	0.54	0.18	200	510	0.25		
FC-2	~bankfull flow	0.18	0.36	0.39	0.44	32	81	0.090		
FC-2	mid flow	0.11	0.23	0.20	0.24	32	81	0.080	step-pool	A4
FC-2	low flow	0.060	0.14	0.08	0.20	32	81	0.053		
ESL-7	~bankfull flow	0.25	0.53	0.97	0.39	84	174	0.129		
ESL-7	mid flow	0.23	0.48	0.86	0.32	84	174	0.120	cascade	B3a
ESL-7	low flow	0.15	0.32	0.42	0.31	84	174	0.147		
ESL-3	~bankfull flow	0.18	0.51	0.87	0.46	58	151	0.155		
ESL-3	mid flow	0.17	0.49	0.80	0.36	58	151	0.159	cascade	B3a
ESL-3	low flow	0.14	0.36	0.42	0.29	58	151	0.141		
ESL-8	~bankfull flow	0.23	0.48	0.91	0.38	70	172	0.139		
ESL-8	mid flow	0.21	0.44	0.78	0.33	70	172	0.122	step-pool	A3
ESL-8	low flow	0.16	0.33	0.48	0.26	70	172	0.129		
RC-1b	high flow	0.28	----	----	0.92	150	330	0.36		
RC-1b	mid flow	0.21	----	----	0.34	150	330	0.36	step-pool	A3a+
RC-1b	low flow	0.09	----	----	0.20	150	330	0.36		
ESL-1	~bankfull flow	0.25	0.57	0.99	0.35	52	156	0.182	step-pool	B3a
ESL-1	mid flow	0.20	0.46	0.70	0.26	52	156	0.207		
RC-3	high flow	0.31	----	1.09	0.51	220	480	0.29		
RC-3	mid flow	0.20	----	0.94	0.31	220	480	0.29	cascade	A3a+
RC-3	low flow	0.12	----	0.57	0.29	220	480	0.29		
ESL-9	~bankfull flow	0.25	0.52	0.92	0.36	62	153	0.163		
ESL-9	mid flow	0.20	0.42	0.65	0.27	62	153	0.162	step-pool	B3a
ESL-9	low flow	0.17	0.35	0.47	0.23	62	153	0.178		
ESL-2	~bankfull flow	0.25	0.53	1.00	0.35	7	70	0.192		
ESL-2	mid flow	0.20	0.41	0.68	0.30	7	70	0.156	step-pool	B3a
ESL-2	low flow	0.16	0.33	0.47	0.18	7	70	0.176		
ESL-4	~bankfull flow	0.26	0.53	0.99	0.34	68	173	0.182		
ESL-4	mid flow	0.26	0.52	0.97	0.27	68	173	0.172	step-pool	B3a
ESL-4	low flow	0.17	0.34	0.50	0.23	68	173	0.163		
FC-6	~bankfull flow	0.12	0.26	0.17	0.50	49	95	0.134		
FC-6	mid flow	0.07	0.18	0.09	0.24	49	95	0.126	cascade	A4a+
FC-6	low flow	0.05	0.12	0.04	0.15	49	95	0.137		
ESL-5	~bankfull flow	0.24	0.51	1.20	0.30	53	143	0.259		
ESL-5	mid flow	0.22	0.48	1.09	0.29	53	143	0.236	step-pool	B3a
ESL-5	low flow	0.15	0.34	0.59	0.20	53	143	0.221		
FC-3	~bankfull flow	0.19	0.41	0.55	0.32	12	50	0.124		
FC-3	mid flow	0.11	0.24	0.24	0.15	12	50	0.108	step-pool	B4a
FC-3	low flow	0.07	0.15	0.12	0.13	12	50	0.112		
FC-4	~bankfull flow	0.21	0.44	0.48	0.34	47	95	0.171		
FC-4	mid flow	0.12	0.26	0.21	0.22	47	95	0.151	step-pool	B3a
FC-4	low flow	0.09	0.21	0.14	0.13	47	95	0.121		
RC-5	high flow	0.24	----	----	0.27	290	630	0.57	cascade	A2a+
RC-5	low flow	0.11	----	----	0.15	290	630	0.57		

APPENDIX B: Measured Values, Single Discharge Reaches

Reach	Reference	Date	Slope (m/m)	n	f	V (m/s)	Q (m^3/s)	W, meas. (m)
Porter-11	Wohl and Wilcox 2004	1/2003	0.013	0.057	0.44	0.68	----	5.1
Buena Esperanza-A	Comiti et al. 2008	2/2006	0.022	0.059	0.50	0.77	0.40	4.4
Porter-4	Wohl and Wilcox 2004	1/2003	0.026	0.074	0.74	0.74	----	1.6
Buena Esperanza-C	Comiti et al. 2008	2/2006	0.023	0.081	0.94	0.56	0.53	4.2
Porter-6	Wohl and Wilcox 2004	1/2003	0.047	0.091	1.1	0.81	----	3.3
Porter-9	Wohl and Wilcox 2004	1/2003	0.036	0.11	1.7	0.57	----	5.4
Porter-8	Wohl and Wilcox 2004	1/2003	0.045	0.13	2.3	0.55	----	5.1
Tres Arroyos-15	Comiti et al. 2008	4/2005	0.028	0.13	2.7	0.31	0.091	3.6
Kowai-8	Wohl and Wilcox 2004	1/2003	0.064	0.14	3.1	0.40	----	2.6
Camp-5	Wohl and Wilcox 2004	3/2003	0.100	0.19	6.4	0.35	----	6.7
Camp-2	Wohl and Wilcox 2004	3/2003	0.16	0.22	8.6	0.38	----	6.0
Kellogg (Lower)	MacFarlane and Wohl 2003	7/1999	0.061	0.25	11	0.18	----	2.1
Buena Esperanza-E	Comiti et al. 2008	3/2006	0.076	0.25	8.3	0.37	0.18	4.6
Tres Arroyos-14	Comiti et al. 2008	4/2005	0.072	0.26	11	0.26	0.070	3.0
Buena Esperanza-G	Comiti et al. 2008	3/2006	0.10	0.27	10	0.39	0.19	2.8
SF Mashel (Lower)	MacFarlane and Wohl 2003	7/1999	0.051	0.31	16	0.17	----	2.6
Camp-7	Wohl and Wilcox 2004	2/2003	0.19	0.34	20	0.27	----	2.7
Lost	Curran and Wohl 2003	7/1997	0.12	0.35	19	0.25	----	2.3
Kowai-1	Wohl and Wilcox 2004	2/2003	0.18	0.36	23	0.25	----	3.2
Spine	Curran and Wohl 2003	7/1997	0.12	0.38	27	0.16	----	1.5
SF Mashel (Upper)	MacFarlane and Wohl 2003	7/1999	0.12	0.45	40	0.12	----	1.3
Busywild	MacFarlane and Wohl 2003	7/1999	0.083	0.48	41	0.12	----	1.4
Caterpillar	MacFarlane and Wohl 2003	7/1999	0.14	0.52	59	0.09	----	0.94
McLaine	Curran and Wohl 2003	6/1997	0.18	0.27	45	0.21	----	2.0
Tacoma (Upper)	MacFarlane and Wohl 2003	7/1999	0.099	0.65	71	0.11	----	2.3
Hard	Curran and Wohl 2003	7/1997	0.093	0.74	76	0.13	----	3.2
Tres Arroyos-10	Comiti et al. 2008	3/2005	0.153	0.87	118	0.11	0.067	5.3
Bear	Curran and Wohl 2003	6/1997	0.11	0.96	152	0.079	----	1.70

Reach	W, bankfull (m)	L (m)	R (m)	Fr	D_{50} (mm)	D_{84} (mm)	σ_z (m)	Stream Type M&B (1997)	Rosgen
Porter-11	7.2	56.7	0.2	----	150	164	0.039	plane-bed	C3
Buena Esperanza-A	----	21.5	0.17	0.72	----	223	0.084	plane-bed / step-pool	B3
Porter-4	2.7	34.8	0.2	----	142	235	0.115	plane-bed / step-pool	E3b
Buena Esperanza-C	----	17.2	0.16	0.37	----	113	0.232	plane-bed / riffle-glide	B3
Porter-6	5.6	55.9	0.2	----	155	410	0.209	plane-bed / step-pool	B3a
Porter-9	8.1	53.6	0.2	----	60	207	0.149	plane-bed / step-pool	B4
Porter-8	9.3	49.9	0.2	----	109	245	0.195	plane-bed / step-pool	B3a
Tres Arroyos-15	----	36.9	0.12	0.35	----	151	0.179	pool-riffle / step-pool	B3
Kowai-8	5.0	33	0.8	----	60	180	0.128	plane-bed / step-pool	B4a
Camp-5	13.0	47	1.4	----	450	1350	0.396	cascade	A2
Camp-2	23.0	46	0.6	----	300	1000	0.478	step-pool	A2a+
Kellogg (Lower)	----	48	0.076	----	111	294	0.142	step-pool	B3a
Buena Esperanza-E	----	23.4	0.19	0.36	----	260	0.122	cascade	B3a
Tres Arroyos-14	----	50.4	0.13	0.28	----	341	0.263	step-pool / cascade	A3
Buena Esperanza-G	----	16.9	0.19	0.30	----	336	0.192	step-pool	A3a+
SF Mashel (Lower)	----	58	0.11	----	137	256	0.143	step-pool	B3a
Camp-7	3.5	30	0.5	----	430	910	0.281	step-pool	A2a+
Lost	3.3	54	0.13	----	65	187	0.256	step-pool	A3a+
Kowai-1	10.3	46	0.1	----	240	535	0.358	step-pool	A3a+
Spine	2.2	53	0.077	----	33	123	0.390	step-pool / cascade	B3a
SF Mashel (Upper)	----	52	0.060	----	108	223	0.172	step-pool	B3a
Busywild	----	56	0.085	----	158	284	0.161	step-pool	A3
Caterpillar	----	55	0.047	----	111	239	0.334	step-pool	B3a
McLaine	3.3	48	0.14	----	80	193	0.521	step-pool	A3a+
Tacoma (Upper)	----	51	0.11	----	158	416	0.349	step-pool	B3a
Hard	4.8	61	0.18	----	87	203	0.348	step-pool / cascade	A3
Tres Arroyos-10	----	32	0.13	0.11	----	143	0.599	step-pool	A3a+
Bear	3.1	74	0.11	----	101	216	0.233	step-pool	A3a+

United States Department of Agriculture
Forest Service
Rocky Mountain Research Station